A Voice Came Down the Mountain

A Voice Came Down The Mountain

*Ana's words, not her bullets,
revolutionized Mayan lives
...and mine*

Terry Winckler

Also by Terry Winckler
Tule Town

ISBN Paperback: 979-8-9881449-3-9
Library of Congress Number: 2024915022

Editors: David Lewis, Laura Oda, Mike Meenan
Layout/Formatting: Sarah Lahay
Cover Design: Tito Alfredo Palacios
Photos: front cover of volcanoes Atitlan and Toliman by the author; back cover of author by Chris Freck; "On The Volcano" photos by Laura Oda; Cunen boys and the poet by Michael Plyler; volcano topped with lightning courtesy of Sergio Montufar; all other photos supplied by author

Author website: terrywinckler.com

TerWin Publishing LLC
Printed in United States of America

*In memory of Capitana Ana and all those who
fought to empower the Maya people*

*In homage to Father Greg, Margaret and Tom
Melville, and other clerics who didn't just pray*

*In gratitude to Harris Done and AYUDA for
introducing me to the Maya world*

Author's Note

This greatest story of my life began during the Cold War when the United States and Soviet Union avoided nuclear self-annihilation by throwing elbows at each other in places like Vietnam and Guatemala, where I first arrived in 1972 at age 25 as a volunteer aid worker in a poor Mayan village. Told through my eyes as they gained wisdom over decades, the story focuses not on the sweep of human events but on how we experience them — one at a time. One afflicted village among hundreds, one grieving father among thousands, one murder among hundreds of thousands, one village poet who taught me how to see into the heart of Maya existence. And high atop a volcano, one tiny band of revolutionaries captained by a woman who vowed *ni un paso atras* — not one step backwards until all Mayans are free from the bondage of centuries. The story opens near its climax in 2018 when I returned to the volcano looking for her.

Terry Winckler in 1972 and 2018

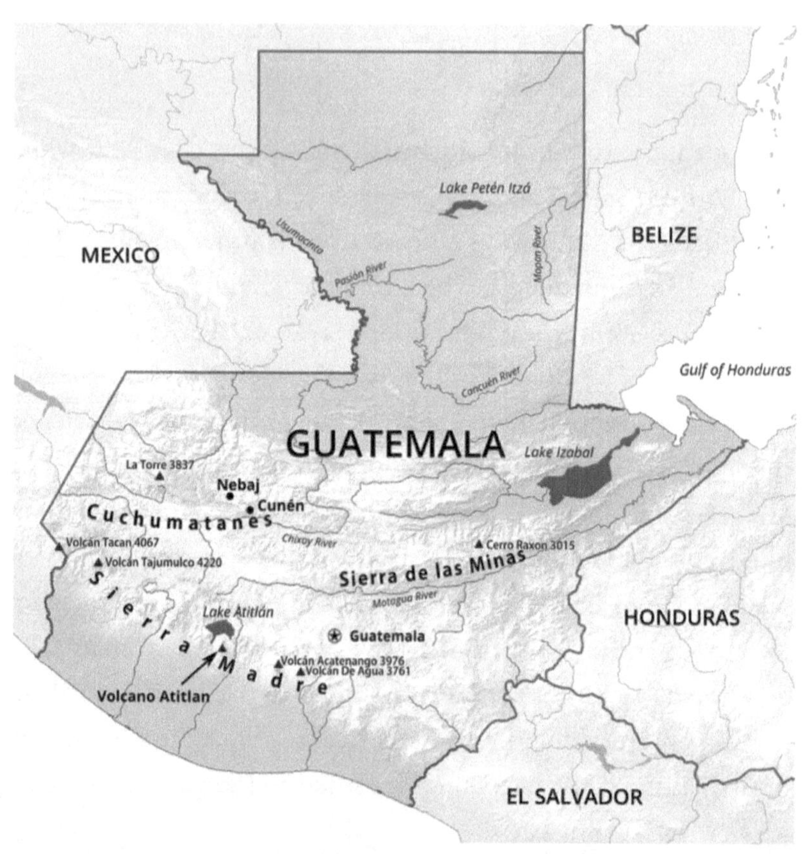

Map1: Guatemala

Contents

Looking For Ana

2018

Gaspar disappeared into the neblina

On The Volcano

"Hoooayyyyy!"

If lightning had a tenor voice, this was it, striking down through the mist to where we sit on logs at a junction of trails worn deep into black soil by many feet over many years among cornstalks, coffee plants, and avocado trees.

"It is Gaspar!" cries Alejandra, rising so quickly that the baby at her nipple drops into the cloth sling across her chest. Lean, tough Gaspar, a Mayan farmer from the village at the base of this volcano, left us here 30 minutes ago while he went searching alone up a steep trail and vanished into the neblina — a mysterious, wistful, almost living creation of wetness blown upslope from the Pacific Ocean to where the coolness of altitude enchants it into a fog like no other. Here at the junction it is the soft steam of a spa, but up there it could be a blinding storm or shifty as the veil of a Persian dancer, constantly moody and a perfect cover for ambush. We thought Gaspar was lost in it.

Lost? Hard to believe. Volcano Atitlan has been his backyard since *he* was a baby carried in a mother's sling. He played upon it as a boy, worked its fields as a man, and when the revolution came, guided guerrillas against soldiers creeping up its side.

Gaspar points out ambush site

"We killed 41 soldiers here," he boasted at one point on our trek, gesturing toward a slanted plain of thick, low-lying bush where he and his compañeros hid with rifles as the enemy stalked, and my skin shivered at the memory of how I had once run openly across this volcano during the revolution, no doubt watched by hidden eyes.

Gaspar's body is classic male Mayan, compact with muscled calves dropping out of heavy, knee-length cotton pantaloons embroidered with purple stripes and a garden of multicolored flowers. Everything about him is muscled, except those eyes that beam like dark searchlights from his sun-roughened face. He is the perfect example of a man born to roam this volcanic land along with wild creatures who crawl and slither and fly — like the ridiculously beautiful quetzal bird Gaspar pointed out lumbering across the sky burdened by its long, luxurious tail.

"HOOOOOAYYYY!!"

Gaspar's suddenly closer voice wrenches our eyes upslope to see him trot out of the mist, breathless and grinning.

"I have found her!"

Ana.

The woman I ran through a minefield to meet on this volcano 33 years before. Bold, beautiful Capitana Ana who stood with her lover Comandante Pancho as they led guerrillas against the genocidal army her father served in. Who opened my heart with vast eyes and filled it with two words that will always pulse within me: *Somos iguales* — We are all equals. Words that echo those at the heart of the U.S. Declaration of Independence and help explain why Ana chose the revolution over her young daughter, the now-grown-up mother who walks with me, pouring kisses and cuddles upon her baby...of the kind she could only dream about as a lonely child.

"Come," Gaspar says, and we follow him into the neblina, upwards toward a place so secret and sacred that only a chosen few may ever visit. The place where Ana's ashes are buried.

We are absorbed into a mystery Alejandra keeps hinting at without saying much about because, it seems, she wants the answer to reveal itself, although I don't even know what the question is. Shhh, she says when I probe, reminding me that she had lived her whole life before discovering what I will find in just minutes. How alluring to stumble along through that fog-wrapped puzzle, but also frustrating because, if not for the neblina, my eyes could gaze east at the far-off spine of Guatemala — the towering Cuchumatanes Mountains where I first spied this volcano on a sweet night five decades ago.

I was gawking in the way young people do when they begin exploring outside of their birth-world and are dazzled by appearances, especially such natural beauty as Guatemala's. It was the time in between pulses of a revolution that had flared briefly in the 1960s before it was crushed and went into seething hibernation within Guatemala's many hiding places, invisibly reseeding itself among Mayan people in jungles, forests, mountains, and volcanoes, and among mixed-blood young intellectuals in the big city. A tutored eye could see that it wasn't just wind rustling leaves in places where rebellion grew, but my eyes were uneducated and, as a village poet would lament when I returned years later after revolution had erupted openly, could not see the truth of his people's anguish. It is he who put me on the road to find that truth...the road to Ana, who, like me, had first gone into those mountains with hope that she could help Mayans improve their lives. Unlike me, though, Ana had vision the poet might applaud — and what she saw transformed her into a rebel on a volcano, while I shrugged my shoulders at the futility of it all and hitchhiked home to the United States along the same route migrants take today.

"Come," Gaspar urges as I fall behind, wobbling on a bad left knee and wandering through mists of memory.

A Time of
In-Between

March, 1973

On The Shangri-La Road

Ahhh, what a night to be me, running — dancing, practically — up a steep road toward a full moon rising over the mountain's edge. My swinging left arm brushed against tree vines, making their tangled shadows come alive in the lunar glow which created them, while far below on my right spread the hilly vastness of Guatemala to a distant horizon of volcanoes stabbing up like dragon's teeth into lightning-filled clouds.

Twenty miles of mountain road lay under my feet.

I had never run such a distance.

I was exhilarated.

And free.

Puffs of smoke — not smoke but the cast-off dust from this mountain — kicked up as I took long, swift strides with my long, thin legs and laughed at an unexpected thought. *If the army doctors could only see me now, could see how that left knee moves like its brother to make me a gazelle, would they send me off to fight with others of my age in that hell of Vietnam? They sent everyone else, it seemed, but not me.*

"My left knee bends backwards. I was hit by a linebacker one year and by a car the next," I told army doctors after being called up for a draft physical. "The car wrapped the leg around my neck."

"Show us," one doctor demanded — the same one who had just condemned a polio victim to fight in jungles. The poor kid stood on bones wrapped in skin with little evidence of muscle, yet the doctor sneered, "You can't dodge the draft on them things, son." He slammed down a well-worn stamp that designated the boy as 1-A, like the blue butcher's mark on a side of prime beef, except he didn't look prime.

My skinny legs shook as the doctor barked out commands to drop my pants and do knee bends. His eyes widened when the left knee went backwards, and I heard the soft slap of a stamp they rarely used because my generation was dying fast in the jungles and the generals needed every limping one of us. "Go in that room," the doctor said, where a Red Cross nurse sighed as she read what the stamp meant, took my hands, and said she had bad news.

My heart paused.

"The Army doesn't want you."

Whaaat!?

In an apologetic tone, as if she was denying my birthright to fight communism, she explained: "They've classified you 1-H."

A winning number! My number. But what exactly was the prize?

"It means you won't be drafted until bombs start falling on L.A."

I danced on that wiggly knee with a heart of joy past hundreds of scared boys the Army *did* want, onto the sunny streets of Los Angeles, and from that moment on quit worrying about communist Vietnam as a threat to me, but kept my belief that communism was a threat to mankind. I had been raised in a Catholic family to hate and fear communism because its God-killing virus had infected Eastern Europe and China, and now threatened to engulf all of Asia, Central America, and the United States, too, if we didn't take a stand. I don't remember if I thanked God for letting that car knock me out of going to Vietnam because he had other plans for me, but that's how I used to think, thanks to my Irish-Catholic mother and all the nuns and priests who trained me in that belief.

"God works in mysterious ways," mom assured me in the hospital where I lay writhing in pain for a month. Before the car accident, I had spent a year in a seminary run by Maryknoll — a missionary order whose priests were kicked out of China during its revolution and told me horror stories about Mao Tse Tung's attack on religion. I absorbed books by Tom Dooley, a good Catholic boy and Navy doctor in Vietnam who wrote about seeing chopsticks pounded into peasants' ears by communist invaders. I held dear the warnings about communism from that good Catholic President John Kennedy after he stared down Russia over missiles in Castro's communist Cuba, and nodded my head prayerfully as priests thundered from their pulpits and the Pope dictated from his balcony about the communist scourge pouring down upon the planet like red paint from a bucket in space.

Don't laugh when I tell you the devil's army was coming to get us. That message bound many of us together during the early years of America's longest war, until hundreds of thousands of angry dissenters were marching against it by 1973

— but not me. I was confused about the war, not my country, and war protesters sounded like they were against America itself. What's the difference, they said, between us napalming peasants in jungles and the Nazis gassing Jews in concentration camps? I knew the difference, why the fuck didn't they? War is hell but sometimes necessary. It's how we got rid of the redcoats, eliminated slavery, and kept Germany and Japan from making *us* slaves. Wasn't my generation paying attention in history classes? The Nazis blew up my uncle Jack on his way to church and shot torpedoes into my father's ships. We weren't Nazis. We were good people with good intentions in the best country on Earth.

In time, I would hear whispers of truth not taught in most schools of that era — especially in the South where I was raised— about how war had allowed us to have the best country in the world, and that our forefathers used its weapons to slaughter the Indians so that we could have their land for slaves to work on. It's what the Spanish Conquistadors did in Guatemala nearly 500 years ago and what modern conquerors were still doing as I showed up — something I didn't know on the night I ran in moonlight from the weavers' village of Nebaj. It was many years before the whispers became a shout that drowned out the national anthem singing in my young heart and forced me to see my country and this country and the rest of the world in a different light. And made me pray instead of pledge when my hand was over my heart. I adored my sweet land of liberty and would have served in Vietnam instead of running off to Canada as many did or doing what my ultra-right wing buddy did to dodge the draft — marry a woman he didn't love and knock her up to have a kid he didn't want and, then, in an act of utter insurance against being drafted, go to divinity school to become a minister in a religion he didn't believe, then rant against those who protested the war. And so — in the very month protesters finally convinced Nixon to pull our troops from Vietnam — I was guilt-free and happy as I ran in the moonlight. And why not? I had dangled my leg patriotically and they didn't want it, so I was running on it up that mountain road after visiting one of the most wondrous places on Earth.

———————

A chicken bus had taken me over the mountain from the village of Cunén to the village of Nebaj early that morning, but though the bus was funky and colorful and smelly and loud and jouncy, I didn't really notice because my heart was focused on our destination. Everything I heard about Nebaj — even its location high in the mountains — convinced me I was heading to the legendary Shangri-La. Nebaj surely was its real-life embodiment, a tranquil world of soft-voiced Mayan women whose fingers played weaving looms like musical instruments.

Of course, anything would seem wondrous after those first hard months in Cunén. I had come as a volunteer aid worker to cure tuberculosis, but when that turned into the greatest fiasco of my life, I picked up a shovel and began learning how to be an *effective* volunteer even as I learned the harshest lesson of all...you can help people endure difficult circumstances, but changing the circumstances is unimaginably difficult. My village was plain and poor and for all who lived there, including me, a place of unending hard work. A fellow named Morse was the volunteers' manager and the sun was his clock. If it shined, you worked. But he also was a devout Mormon who revered the day of rest, so on that Sunday morning — with his blessing and a warning — I hopped on the bus to Nebaj, promising to be back in time for the morrow's toil.

"Make sure you do. We're building a school."

Morse was a worthy man who taught me a great deal more than hard work. He was the first person to take me up a volcano — the one named Fuego that exploded many years later, killing hundreds — to look into its hot, red throat as it burped up boulders the size of Volkswagens. Morse gave me the courage to do it, and I am certain that his inspiration gave extra momentum to my legs 12 years later amid revolution when I came back to go up Ana's volcano. There was something about this man, something he never spoke of, that made him stand tall in my spine. Many years later, after Morse was dead, I discovered the secret and was humbled.

But on the day I went to Nebaj, Morse was just a pain in the ass I was happy to see in the rear-view mirror of that old bus, called a chicken bus because people bring all kinds of animals to market on them. It took me on the 20-mile wriggle out of Cunén along the same mountain ridge I would run back on that night. We ambled along peaceably, my head lolling to the easy bouncing roll of the journey until I awoke with a gasp when a switchback took us head-on toward the edge of a dropoff and then twisted back to the mountain side where we turned left, tipping downward into a valley.

And there lay the lustrous Nebaj, exactly as described in "The Lost Horizon":

"The floor of the valley, hazily distant,
welcomed the eye with greenness....
It was, indeed, a strange and half-incredible sight."

Surrounded by forested mountain palisades — as seen through my fantasy-drugged eyes — Nebaj dazzled. Its many whitewashed and variously colored buildings reflected the sun as it came over the peaks and flashed the village's brilliance. *Hurry,* I silently urged the bus driver, but he navigated the difficult road slowly, through potholes the depth of bathtubs, around little boulders that had rolled off the mountain, and carefully down steep stretches of slippery gravel. I exhaled with relief when the road finally leveled out for a grand, honking entrance through acres of color.

It was market day.

Mayans from throughout the high aldeas had walked down into the village center with hand-wrought goods and foods they arrayed upon the main street sidewalks, and filled up every connecting small road and alleyway. I strolled the bigger streets, marveling at the plentitude that so contradicted the plain poverty of my village. Hand-woven baskets crowded the streets, overflowing with wheelbarrows of yellow and purple bananas, the greenest beans, the reddest peppers; herbal scents teased my nose, along with the sting of chilis and the stink of garlic; and strewn about were gourds long and fat and gnarly with what looked like plague-afflicted cheeks.

But that which truly gave Nebaj its reputation as Shangri-La wasn't at foot level, nor even much in evidence on the main street. The glory of Nebaj flew above in side streets; array after array of weavings that reminded me of fluttering prayer flags criscrossing the streets of Tibet. I plunged in among them, my head caressed by soft blouses and the rough texture of skirt fabric loomed by the famed women weavers who every day sat doing endlessly precise shuttling upon backstrap looms so that they could come down on market day with artistry for sale. I pushed slowly through fabrics hung like wash on long lines that stretched between support poles. Hidden from view far below at my feet, the weavers spoke up to me from where they sat, their hummingbird voices hovering among thickets of woven beauty as they twittered in Spanish.

"Look, senor, how beautiful this corte would look upon your esposa."

"Not so expensive, senor American, this blouse my little daughter spent so many hours making with her little fingers and her tiny needle."

"How can you pass up this lovely belt that will hug your waist like a lover."

Having not so much money and being too overwhelmed to even know what to buy, I kept stumbling along until I met my first alleyway and staggered to a stop. Here in this narrow corridor hung treasure: weavings of such artistry that even my clumsy eye could tell the difference between these and all of the ones I had previously admired. I gazed upon a single beauty — a wide belt richly decorated by talented, caring fingers and long enough to wrap perhaps three times around the thin waist of a young bride — for it was a wedding belt.

This was all explained to me by the tall and regal Mayan woman who held the belt in her upturned palms as if she was the Virgin herself offering a celestial garment. Her eminence was swathed in red offset by bits of every other color. Most impressive was the mound of woven and braided hair that wrapped around her head with a hand-wrought cotton band of colors designed so that it seemed alive. Her sweet voice and coffee brown eyes seduced me forward.

I lifted the belt from her palms and raised it to marvel at woven splashes of gold, maroon, green, red, indigo, white.

No. Upon examination they were rabbits with white bodies and red eyes, or black bodies with gray eyes. White cat faces stared with green eyes and red noses, or were they skulls? No, they must be two-legged creatures with golden breasts and green hearts, and dog heads with the bodies of green and white alligators. Wolves with golden snouts and black mouths howled at me. The creatures played or glared from a field of diamonds and X's, vertical rectangles and horizontal lines — moving up and down the belt with colors that interacted and offset each other, all underlain by stripes of red, white and black that ran the whole length of the belt, which tapered off at each end with all those threads knotted. I closed my eyes and imagined a mother's eyes getting teary as she helped a daughter encircle her young waist with this belt until the tapers came together at her side. I wondered what kind of knot they tied to keep the corte secure, and whether it was meant to untie easily on that special night.

I must have the belt!

"Twenty, senor," the weaver said.

I have exactly 20 quetzals! But...it's all that I have for the next month, so buying the belt means I will not be able to buy cigarettes — even at two per penny — nor bits of candy.

Worth it!

"No, senor," she said gently. "Twenty *dollars*."

D-dollars? My yearning, disappointed gaze found sympathy in hers.

Usually, in the tug-of-war of market day, the seller comes back with a lower price, but this was Nebaj, among the most famous weaving towns in the Americas. Though hard to get to, it had been found by art lovers from around the world, who were everywhere talking in various tongues as they bought weaving masterpieces at close to the price offered with little haggling.

"Que lastima, señor...the price is 20 dollars."

I handed it back with a sigh, consoling myself that at least I will be able to smoke.

"Adios, senora."

"Que le vaya bien."

But all was not lost. A poor boy such as I knew how to buy with his eyes, and off I went on a spree of glance-purchasing among alleys that took me all over Nebaj. So absorbed was I that I didn't heed the passage of time until Indian women started packing for their long treks back up the mountain with mountains of unsold goods balanced on their heads. The sun was leaving fast. Time for me to go as well, but the ticket seller had bad news.

"Sorry, señor, the last bus for Cunén just left. The next one is tomorrow at noon."

Oh, no. Morse is gonna kill me. Our work day starts at dawn. We're building a school.

"How far to Cunén?"

Twenty miles!? There are nine hours until dawn. If I walk, I can just make it. But I got lost and by the time I found the main road I only had eight hours. *I better trot.*

Though I was young and tall and lean and made for distance running despite that wiggly knee, my lungs thought otherwise, having been so often punished by cigarette smoke. They rebelled as I started to lift my legs faster. They coughed and wheezed during the first few hundred yards as the road steepened, and I was uncertain that this was possible. But in those moments, the full moon started peeking over the mountain's edge far up ahead where the road seemed to level off, and bathed me in healing light. The coughing ebbed, the pace picked up, the moon tugged me along as it does the tide, and from behind I sensed the magic of Nebaj lifting me, urging my legs to move even quicker until I was actually running and happy about it, leaping atop those little boulders the bus had dodged, and laughing to see my moon-cast shadow run with me across the rugged mountainside. My heart and feet and lungs were partners in this best run of my life.

"The whole body moved in a single rhythm...
the lungs, no longer discrete and automatic,
were disciplined to harmony with mind and limb."
—THE LOST HORIZON

Suddenly, other runners came off the mountain through the tangled tree vines and on to the road toward me in a column, carrying torches, and — while we were all surprised — none of us altered our movement and swiftly passed by, glancing into each others' eyes, and then they disappeared. Not one of their hard, brown faces had returned my smiles. *Was it a dream? Who were these other runners of the night? Should I be afraid?* Afraid of what? A guy at the U.S. embassy had warned me about seven "commie" guerrillas who entered Guatemala from Mexico a few months before I showed up, but told me not to worry because they had disappeared into a jungle full of hungry jaguars and hadn't been seen since — at least by his eyes — and both of us grinned in shared ignorance, unaware that those seven guerrillas were swiftly moving through the forested heart of Guatemala, whispering as they passed through Mayan hamlets, their words breezing ear to ear with a message of hope for people who had suffered centuries of cruelty wrought by invaders. Your time has come, they said, and people came out of their mud houses to listen. It was the time in-between pulses of revolution crushed years before in jungles to the east and resurrected by this stealthy handful of revolutionaries who were building support for what they hoped would become a massive Mayan uprising. By the time I came running, they had reached Cotzal, a village two mountain peaks and a valley away — perhaps a hard day's foot travel to here along the guerrilla highway of canyons, animal trails, and river channels. If I had known, I might have imagined their whispers amid breezes rustling the forest, but if I had known I might not have come to Guatemala, let alone run at night on this route that Conquistador horses had galloped along 400 years before as they, too, headed toward Cunèn. There was much I didn't know in those days when my eyes looked at everything and saw little; in the time of my own in-between. "You don't know how to see, Terry," the village poet will tell me 12 years from now, but that solemn moment was so far from this one of wonder.

I kept running to that point on the road where all of Guatemala seemed laid out before me. Far off to the west, clouds gripped the pointed tops of that volcanic mountain range and lightning burst like artillery shells among the peaks. Though thunder cannot travel such distance, I knew its bone-rattling power and felt its silence as clouds seethed in a scene from mythology — of war among the gods played on this grand stage, and I was in the balcony agog as the opera sang to my imagination.

> *"It makes me realize how lucky I was to miss the War."*
> —THE LOST HORIZON

In this time of gathering storm, as Churchill had described the moments before World War II, my young eyes saw only mystery and magic even as rebellion brewed down there in the big city among young intellectuals like the future Capitana Ana. While I was learning to love Guatemala's beauty on this mountain, they were learning to hate Guatemala's historic mal-treatment of Mayan people. While I was lost among the weavings, they were discovering truth about the weavers and campesinos and their permanently difficult lives in Nebaj,

Cunén and villages throughout these high mountains — lives bound to rocky, steep land that barely fed them, and sometimes didn't. In years to come, I would learn that brutal tactics used against peasants in Vietnam were being taught by U.S. advisors for use against the peasants of Guatemala. It was not pretty truth, and as the semesters passed Ana and many classmates started planning how to keep that past and this present from becoming the future. But what did I know about any of this in this time before outrage boiled over into open revolution, before civil war soaked these mountains — and that Shangri-la behind me — red with the blood of Mayan people I had walked among, laughed with, worked with, got drunk with, and failed to see as Ana would.

> *"The first quarter-century of your life was doubtless lived under the cloud of being too young for things... There will come a time when you will age like others."*
>
> —THE LOST HORIZON

The full moon beckoned me away from drama to the joy of running. My feet flew through quiet, sleeping hamlets of mud/stick homes with fronds for roofs, past a makeshift soccer field built on the flattest spot they could find but still angled and steep, and I remembered passing by here in daylight when the boys played hard but disciplined. They dared not kick their only soccer ball off the mountain for they could not afford another. I outran a dog whose bark echoed in front of me, and pretended to navigate by a lone bright star. I was alone and happy on a mountain soaked in mystical, milky goodness, and so the run went until near sunrise at a fork on the mountain where the road falls right to Sacapulas and left to Cunén. I saved the right fork for another trek weeks later that I would write a song about. Left was tonight's course. Hundreds of feet below, the whitewashed old mission church glowed in the mixed light of waning moon and rising sun. This morning, as every morning, its steps will be swept by the old man Diego, who taught me how to make adobe. With the moon setting to my back and the pre-dawn glowing on my face, I happily raced down the mountainside and beat the sun home, but I was not earlier than the young Mayan cook already stoking the wood-fired oven. We teased each other with taunts.

"*Mal hombre*!" she yelled at me. Bad man.

"*Mala mujer!*" I yelled back. Bad woman.

My run ended in laughter, until I saw Morse staring at me with his hands on his hips.

"So, you made it after all," he said.

Is he smiling?

"Let's get to work."

A Time of Rebellion

The 1970s

The Asp

As I returned to the task of helping impoverished Mayans cope with their lives, students at the University of San Carlos huddled over plans to revolutionize Mayan lives, while a deadly presence slithered among them with the invisible ears of a snake.

There was rarely a warning when the snake struck, more like an asp than a rattler. Students and professors simply "disappeared" — grabbed night or day on the streets or from their homes or as they strode the campus. Their mutilated corpses would sometimes show up in the city dump, where entire Mayan families lived, combing through garbage to survive, but many others simply vanished and are presumed dead. If there were witnesses, a rarity, they would speak of men driving white vehicles with dark windows who opened doors and snatched victims. Hundreds of students and professors died in such ways.

This is how the ruling class dealt with rebelliousness at the University of San Carlos, located in the very heart of Guatemala City where business, government, and army leaders lived. With its Marxist-tinged curriculum, the university was a big left thumb in their eye. It seemed an odd curriculum for a school founded in 1676 as a Spanish Catholic college in what was then "The Kingdom of Guatemala." Two hundred years later, it was renamed the National University of Guatemala and started developing a more progressive approach. In 1944, amidst a world war eventually won by democracies, its students helped overthrow the latest dictator and replaced him with a man named Arévalo, the country's first democratically elected president, but they were powerless six years later when the U.S. CIA faked a revolution that sent the country's next president fleeing. A dictator who danced to the tune of U.S. political and business interests replaced him, ending "The Spring" of Guatemalan democracy. After that, the ruling class began putting its students into newly formed private colleges and universities where they learned capitalism. God knows they tried to quash what continued going on at the university, sometimes with tanks but always with spies who were students or acted like them, invisibly everywhere on campus with hear-all ears — *orejas*.

The ears could be anywhere students gathered, in classrooms listening to lessons on social inequality, in hallways where students babbled with outrage over the just-learned wrongness of their society, perhaps in the food hall where the clatter of dishes wouldn't hide the fervor of revolutionary ideas, and in meeting places where some students were speaking in quiet tones about actual revolution — overheard nonetheless by someone in their midst.

The people out to get you lived behind walls and were protected by the army. They weren't much more than a handful compared to the vaster number of Mayans, but what a handful — 'pure-blooded' European descendants loosely known as criollos. The first one I met was a tall, thin, cream-colored fellow of about 25 who wore gray calfskin boots made in Russia that came up to his knees and had heels that clicked on the stone streets as he strode about surveying his world from a height that I, though much taller, would never possess. He was the oldest son, the scion, of a wealthy family.

"You romanticize these people as if they are so special they aren't even people," he said after I urged him to travel with me to the highlands and meet some wonderful Mayans who lived without doctors or nurses, without adequate food or shelter, shivering without adequate clothes, striving without opportunity.

He wasn't so much haughty as puzzled about my attempt to discomfit him.

Struck numb by the sincerity of his words, I walked away, thinking of how in-bred his attitude was and of how patronizing I suddenly felt by describing the people as quaint and powerless. His people owned the country's wealth and had for hundreds of years, ever since the Spanish rode in on horses and conquered the Maya. In modern times, U.S. business interests joined up with the country's ruling class to grab land from the Mayans and assemble giant corporate fincas growing cane, coffee and bananas. In an agricultural economy, that meant they owned the country. With U.S. government support, they kept the army well-dressed, well-armed, and well-trained. In turn, the army kept them well-protected against the enemy. The enemy, as preached in harmony by the U.S. and Guatemalan governments, was godless communism infecting witless students and hapless Mayans. Not just infecting but convincing them that their generation could reverse 400+ years of inequality.

Through revolution.

And just over the eastern horizon was a shining example.

It seemed so easy, how Fidel Castro did it. He loaded 81 fighters on a leaky boat in Mexico and took off to free Cuba from its brutal past and present. Three years later in 1959, having chased out the U.S.-backed corrupt capitalists, he declared victory.

If Castro can do it...

Farther east, 10,000 miles away, a different kind on inspiration gave them hope. Vietnamese revolutionaries as little and non-white as Mayans were kicking America's ass.

If Ho Chi Minh can do it...

Talk of Fidel and Ho and the martyred revolutionary Che Guevara swirled among students, including in classrooms where revolutionary, socialist and communist philosophies were taught along with history lessons that presented a different set of facts than most students had been exposed to. They were taught about themselves — mostly members of the middle-class called ladinos with mixed Mayan/European blood lines. They learned how they had inherited a colonial economic system based on taking land from Mayans and forcing them to work for free or nearly free on land they once owned. They learned the same lessons that drove that bearded guy in Cuba to take up arms:

"Marxism taught me what my society was...
that society is divided between the rich and the

poor, and that some people subjugate and exploit other people."

— FIDEL CASTRO

The Marxism taught at San Carlos U. had a Guatemala twist. Here, the rich mostly were pale and the poor mostly were dark. Here, it wasn't just a class struggle but ethnic. Here, where the majority racial group was Mayan, almost no one of color could escape the bondage of skin. It seemed obvious but it took the teachings of intellectuals like sociologist Carlos Guzman Bockler and his counterpart Severo Martinez to make it so for young justice seekers at San Carlos. Look at yourselves, they told students. You were born into privilege if not into wealth. Your wealth is the opportunity to rise in the cultural and economic ranks, whereas those with truly brown skin were born to be inferiors within your culture. Thus it has been since the Conquest. If you, as ladinos, want to bring the Maya into your culture of opportunity then you must first acknowledge that you are not so pure as you think. Mayan blood is inside you. They are already you. Embrace them as brothers and sisters. Help them up the same ladder of opportunity you have as a birthright.

No one embraced them more than the woman who cast off her birth name — and birthright — to become one among them.

A Girl Named Sandra

Arturo had a yellow head.

A green body.

And a hatred for the skinny little girl with orphan-sized eyes named Sandra. Arturo, the family parrot, had tasted what lived inside her and flared like a flamethrower whenever she hovered around his perch. Maybe he saw what I did many years later when I looked into the eyes of the warrior she became under a new name — Ana.

As a child, Sandra was quiet and often shy, especially around boys. What a funny trait for someone who one day would lead men into battle. At age 12, she disappeared under the bed when her brother's friends came to play. You can imagine those big eyes looking up from her hiding place. Eyes that over time seemed to look more inward than out as she swam deep into thoughts before surfacing to act in ways that shocked even those who were close to her, like older brother Mario Roberto. She spent years as a guerrilla before he knew.

Her father Egidio was a colonel in the army she came to know much better than she ever knew him. He wasn't at home enough to know, and even when he was Egidio was an island unto himself with his army ideologies in a family of rebellious women. They included the grandmother Eloisa, her daughter Blanca and her children: America, Sandra, Hilda, and their brother Mario Roberto who hewed more to their father in this matriarchal family.

Did they love him?

One day, Egidio plucked a tiny, orange-red seed from a chiltipepe plant. Smaller than the smallest apple seed. Stronger than the hottest habanero. I once tasted the glisten of its juice on the tip of a tine of a fork and winced as if the fork itself stabbed my tongue.

Egidio held the entire seed up to his children between his thumb and forefinger.

"Whoever loves me the most will eat this whole."

Sandra snatched it, ate it, endured it.

An act of love or defiance? If not both, the latter. Sandra was, above all, fearless. Skinny, yes, but those thin legs didn't know how to step backwards when her mind was set. Yet, being practical, she knew how to step aside in the face of a dangerous foe — a tactic taught by the most famous guerrilla of them all, Che Guevara, who wrote in his manual on guerrilla warfare: "... the essential task of the guerrilla fighter is to keep himself from being destroyed."

But Che came into her life long after the parrot.

Arturo was on his perch one day in the kitchen where Sandra and her younger sister Hilda were washing dishes. Usually, Sandra targeted the smaller Hilda when her bullying impulses took over, but this time she only had eyes for the bird and flung hot water at it. The bird screeched with rage, flaring its wings and feathers, forcing her to retreat. What inspiration for a persecuted sister! Hilda waited for a day when Sandra was particularly mean and took the parrot from its perch into Sandra's room, cowing her with its homicidal freak show. She begged forgiveness and vowed never again to harm Hilda.

It seemed a turning point for such a quick learner, but if the incident tempered the bully it had no effect on the boss. At school, Sandra was the one who ordered other students into line, snapping at them like a sergeant major. The grand dame mother had to like that — one of many qualities that made Sandra her favorite. She was the disciplined one who put those big eyes upon page after page of book after book to scoop up scholastic awards. She's the one you saw in school wearing the sash of achievement at graduation ceremonies. The one who, not having a family with money enough to send her through college, earned it with scholarships.

As an antidote to her mean streak, Sandra had a big heart, like her brain. Capable of being a bully, she became a defender of the weak against true bullies. It was good training for someone who absorbed what others did not and processed them in ways that lit a path forward through the Mayan's world of pain to the top of a volcano where she vowed to change their world for the better.

As Sandra's family spoke of her early years, I began to understand her militant compassion. She, like me, had been raised within Catholic schools by nuns and priests who taught that *the poor will always be with us* — as if the poor were endowed by their creator with the genetics of poverty. Helping the poor and downtrodden is why nuns and priests make a vow of poverty, so they can truly be among them, hungering with them for the greater reward to come and helping them to endure their God-given test.

A different set of nuns and priests took hold of Sandra in high school: the Maryknolls, a missionary order from the United States. I spent my first high school year in a Maryknoll seminary, studying to be a priest, but there was a difference between the Marknollers who taught me and those who influenced Ana.

My teachers were old-schoolers who had witnessed the sweep of communist revolutions throughout southeast Asia after World War II and taught a single warning lesson: *beware — communists eliminate religion*, which they saw as using "God" and his rules to control the people so that capitalists could exploit them. They replaced those rules with Marxist dogma that makes all people equal by crushing individuality. Communists , the teachers said, speak about people as "the masses", as if people are merely bits of a bland whole, wearing the same clothes, eating the same food, believing the same things, singing and talking in unison, doing and thinking what they are told by those who know best. Every person part of a gray, ordinary mush. For a person who hated mush, which I frequently ate at the seminary breakfast, it was easy to be repulsed by the mush-makers described by priests, and it was horrifying to think of a society that eliminated God. Without the deity, where's the reward for living a good life or enduring the bad one?

Imagine, Terry, if Mother Teresa and Saint Peter — at the end of lives spent helping the poor endure their bitter lives — simply blipped away with the last heartbeat. No other side. No angelic chorus to wake them up. No hugs from a grateful Jesus. No golden gates or heavenly mansions. Nothing but blip for them and the downtrodden people they taught to endure oppression as the price for paradise. It was one of many such thoughts I fingered like my rosary while walking the seminary grounds with other seminarians, dressed in our identical black cassocks, saying the same prayers bead by bead.

Sandra's high school teachers were the new Maryknollers who came to Central America, saw why revolution was gaining a foothold among Mayan peoples, and decided the people were getting screwed and had been ever since God and Caesar rode in on the same horse during the Conquest. The new Maryknollers, like Father Thomas Melville and Sister Marian Peter, had walked the highlands of Guatemala years before I did. Step by step, they saw how the Mayans struggled to survive. Along with other Catholic clergy, especially Jesuits, they began to understand — step by step — how they were mostly helping these people endure lives of inherited hopelessness, finding with every step that they were part of a system that had evolved to keep the people in their places. Like the Catholic clergy who accompanied the Conquistadores, the Maryknollers were helping the people stay within the fold of what amounted to a state religion: in church, down on the farm, under the thumb. That shared realization swept through Central America and years later would be named "Liberation Theology", but long before then Father Tom had already rebelled against treating the poor as a permanent underclass that must be helped to endure their burden as if a trial from God, and began developing cooperatives among the Mayan to improve their lives — an action seen as communistic by death squads that soon would target organizers like Tom.

Meanwhile, the good nun was coming to similar conclusions after years of teaching privileged upper-class ladina girls at an exclusive high school in Guatemala — Monte Maria (Maryknoll). At some point, she took fair-skinned Girl Scouts on hiking trips up volcanoes, where they observed Mayan peasants working and living in poverty circumstances, and on one trip, accompanied by the leader of FAR, a secret guerrilla group, learned some history about how oppressed the Maya were. This led to consciousness-training programs Sister Mary Peter called "The Crater" after a nearby volcano exploded as her students were outside. Ears to the ground, they heard eruptions gathering force underground as if it was justice preparing its appearance.

Years later, when Tom and Margaret compared notes, they agreed their actions were futile in a rigged political system supported by the U.S. They began rebelling together — against religious vows used as a control mechanism and against a religious/political system that maintained an oppressive status quo. In unison, they secretively met in Mexico with some men plotting to create a new guerrilla group called the EGP — the Guerrilla Army of the Poor. The priest and nun would add to it a Christian element.

Armed? Christian clergy?

"What would you do?" The 90-year-old former nun retorted when I talked to her in 2018. "They were massacring people."

But, before they could act they were kicked out of the country when a spy exposed their plans, and they returned to the U.S. The other conspirators returned to plotting and seven of them eventually crossed into Guatemala in 1972 just months before I came for the first time.

Removed from Maryknoll as well, the now-former priest and nun fully revolted by getting married and raiding a U.S. government draft registry with other draft protesters, stealing records and burning them on a street in Boston. That's how I first encountered their names — in headlines about their anti-Vietnam War action. I was horrified. I couldn't believe Maryknollers could do such things. My world shook. It was the year I had been rejected by the draft board for duty in Vietnam.

Meanwhile, in Guatemala, the work they and other revolutionaries had done to teach a different brand of religion and history was attracting army attention. Soldiers swept through the highlands, destroying villages and massacring thousands of Mayans. This early show of revolution was crushed, but its lessons survived to be taught to an emerging generation of middle-class firebrands — Sandra's generation. Her older sister America took the 17-year-old to the Maryknoll program in faraway, rural La Libertad in the Cuchumatanes, where they worked among the native people as teachers, and ate as villagers — sparse amounts of coffee, beans and tortillas — suffering hunger pangs for the first time in their lives. On weekends, hunger inspired their attendance at church, where they could eat the richer fare of priests. They begged their mother to bring food and realized that teaching literacy would not feed the people's permanent hunger.

Sandra fell in love with a tall, fair-skinned American Peace Corps volunteer named Tom — her first love — but at summer's end so, too, ended the romance. "I live in the United States. You live in Guatemala," he told the heart-broken young woman.

She cried all the way into her first year at San Carlos University with its warm, embracing ferment. Having had a broken relationship in my first year of college, it's easy to empathize with Sandra's broken-hearted entrance into college. You're a sack of shredded nerve endings....and vulnerable. In so many ways, the world's unfairness was pressing upon Sandra's heart and mind and moral essence. What a perfect student for philosophies that offered answers.

Imagine being 18-year-old Sandra as she starts trading thoughts about the true nature of Guatemalan society with other young ladino students in that left ventricle that was San Carlos U. in the very heart of Guatemala City. Surely, they compared themselves to the Mayans and realized that their colorless skin was a passport to opportunity. There was a joke in my village of Cunén about how to tell the difference between a Mayan and a ladino: just put on western clothes. They don't make you taller. Your belly isn't fuller. Your skin doesn't change tone. But you feel and look different. More superior. More acceptable. Feel equal, act equal, be equal: the secret of success — if you can find a ladder to climb.

Sandra almost certainly got it. Decades after her death, a Mayan woman wept softly as she spoke of how Sandra — as the guerrilla Ana — came into her village to teach the people, and in particular its women, how to believe in and stand up for themselves.

The skin is just the outside, power is inside where we are all equal — if you believe it, she told them.

How practical of Sandra to absorb the ideas of Bolker and Martinez and put them into action. The kind of thing her close university friend Ovidio was not surprised by. "She was so sensible. She listened carefully to what was taught and looked for ways to implement the teachings."

It's why she chose agronomy — the science of agriculture — as a solution to improve the Mayan people's plight. Hey, the country's economy is founded on agriculture, so if you want to improve their lives, improve how they farm. Just common sense. At La Libertad, she saw the exhausted, rocky, steep plots of land the native people struggled to live on. I saw the same thing in Cunén, although I never saw why they were there in the first place or why they stayed generation after generation. We volunteers were there to help them cope, and our answer to marginal soil was chemical fertilizer. A miracle! After campesinos saw demonstration crops explode in abundance, they all wanted it but it was too expensive and, like drugs, it took more and more to keep the wheat and corn high. It failed to cure the real issues: tired land and too little of it. The best land had long ago been seized by the elite class, sometimes in collusion with U.S. business interests, and turned into vast, rich plantations where campesinos were forced to work hard for little pay. "Mucho trabajo, poco dinero," they joked then, and still do today as they pick crops in U.S. fields, pound nails atop U.S. roofs, and push carriages full of U.S. babies. A campesino in my village came back from a coastal plantation with his right forearm swollen like Popeye's after knicking it with his machete. It blew up with infection. Dorothy, the kindly Mormon volunteer nurse, laid him down in our clinic with an antibiotic drip that poured into him for days as she filled the air with prayer. When his skin burst like that of a roasting pig, she whispered, "I don't think he is going to make it." But the next morning he awoke with a smile. Swelling had retreated. "Thank you, Jesus!" Dorothy cried out with hands raised high and fluttering. The campesino went back to the plantation. Others died. Nothing changed.

Ovidio also was an agronomy major and often studied with Sandra, who he remembers as "a trailblazer - the only woman in our class." Indeed, she was one of only two or three women in all Central America to earn an agronomy degree. They were close, but nothing romantic. Ovidio was a bit older, married, with two kids - and thus was anchored in life and less susceptible to the revolutionary zeal he saw among students all around him, including Sandra. They all were exposed to political thinkers who interpreted Marx through the lens of Guatemala's racial divide — coming to the conclusion that Mayans were virtual slaves. It took a civil war to free slaves in the United States and, increasingly, that's what students like Sandra were considering for their country. But not solid, steady, sober Ovidio who thought the system should be changed not overthrown. In the 70s, before trade unions were targeted by the government for slaughter, he formed a union to improve conditions at the furniture factory he worked at. He and Sandra both won scholarships and often worked on projects together. Sometimes he went to her house.

"She had this crazy parrot," he laughed. It went bonkers whenever they entered its room. He thought the bird was reacting to him, but came to realize it was her fierce nature.

If he had listened more closely to the parrot, maybe he would have seen that Sandra truly was an 'Ana', although he suspected it. "At that age if you knew history and saw the reality of the country, you probably would want to change the world, and everybody tried to do so in their own way."

Sandra went on vacations to different parts of the country such as the jungles of Peten where guerrilla groups were rustling leaves. She invited Ovidio but he had those children, that job. He knew she was up to something but never asked what because too many ears were listening. The less you knew, the less you were likely to reveal if the ears came for you with methods to make you talk. He never talked to anyone about such things at the university. You didn't know who you were talking to.

Pretending ignorance, he watched quietly as students all around him morphed into revolutionaries — the kind Sandra hung out with; rebellious sorts like that fellow Marco who was 25 when she met him at 18. She started drinking coffee with this gentle, caring guy. He wasn't tall and handsome like Tom the Peace Corps guy, just a good guy with ideas that bubbled like hers. They drank a lot of coffee together....coffee cultivated and picked by poor, brown fingers.

From his other dimension, Ovidio saw the disappearances and killing of fellow students. It seemed to start escalating in 1976 with the murder of Alejandro Cojiti, a Mayan who was running to be president of the student union. His death was part of a great extermination plan being carried out around the country against leader types: students, teachers, social workers, priests, dissidents; anyone who appeared to be organizing in support of the Mayan people.

Ovidio stayed on track like most students and graduated into the mainstream world of work. As most did.

Sandra, too, graduated, but she had long before entered her true life's work. Only a few family members — and Marco, whom she married — knew that she had gone underground as an urban collaborator with a new revolutionary group called ORPA, the Revolutionary Organization of the People in Arms, one of four such groups fighting in different parts of the country.

Eventually, atop the volcano, she met Pancho, who came to ORPA by a much different path.

A Boy Named Pedro

"You puta - whore! When you were born in La Frutera hospital I entered the maternity ward and almost fell down. At the first step my foot sank to my ankle on the carpet!"

Uncle Rafa loved telling the story of how Pedro - a boy who would become the guerrilla leader Pancho - was born into luxury on the lands of United Fruit Company, the U.S.-owned business known as "La Frutera" for the bananas it grew on a vast territory of fertile lands, much of it extorted from native people, many of whom were forced to work those lands at low wages. As Pedro recalled:

"The houses we lived in were mansions similar to those erected in the southern United States, equipped with eight domestic employees, a car with a particular line, the Bananera club with its swimming pools, the bowling alley and the first golf course in the whole country. The parties were entertained in the style of the big bands of New Orleans."

Pedro re-told the story to illustrate how privilege didn't automatically blind someone to the plight of poor people. To the contrary, it made him aware of how oppressed the Mayans were after he visited the Mayan highlands and saw their mud/ stick houses and how they were shackled to poor land without hope for a better life. The experience shook him and his student friends.

"For the first time in Guatemala, we had discovered the indigenous world and, unlike the previous Ladino generations, we were moved by a great admiration, a great respect and the conviction that the development of Guatemala had as its main protagonist the Mayan people. We assumed a life commitment with this way of thinking."

"La Frutera" was one of two informal names for United Fruit Company. The other was "El Pulpo" — the octopus — which more accurately depicted the many ways UFC controlled Guatemala. It owned 40 percent of Guatemala's land, was its biggest employer and virtually ran the country. Decade after decade, dictators had blessed the company with free land and political favors in an economic alliance greased with bribes that kept everyone happy except the poor majority Mayans. The banana land had been taken from them. As they protested, the country turned into a police state against them until the dictators were kicked out in 1944 by free elections that installed its first democratically elected president, Juan Jose Arévalo.

Viva, Arévalo! A sensitive man of the people, he began instituting policies favorable to the working class and to the poor. After Arévalo's 6-year term expired, an even-more progressive president, Jacobo Arbenz, was elected and, with the multitudes singing their support, committed political suicide by forcing the banana company to sell back unused land at cheap prices so he could give it it to 500,000 landless peasants. In this time of fervent post-World War II anti-communism, what could be more communistic than taking from the rich and giving to the poor? Never mind that United Fruit was paid exactly what they claimed the land was worth in fraudulent tax filings winked at by previous corrupt administrations.

In 1954 — a year before Pedro's birth — the UFC and the U.S. CIA collaborated to overthrow Arbenz with a fake revolution, using psy-op tactics and U.S. planes dropping dynamite on Guatemala City to create fear as a young doctor named Che Guevara watched...learning to hate the U.S. When Arbenz fled, a U.S.-approved dictator took over, and so ended the last peaceful hope for poor people to have a democracy that represented them. This act of treachery — marketed to the U.S. public as a success in keeping communism out of the Americas — is perhaps the single most important reason why so many Pedros and Sandras of their generation became Panchos and Anas. Their country had been stolen once more by outside powers, and the Mayans remained economic slaves.

I was 7-years-old then and hooked on bananas — as most Americans were. Bite by bite, we helped finance efforts to keep U.S.-friendly dictators in power and poor people poor. Over time it took mouthfuls to buy the bullets, supply the tanks, pay for the training of military forces, and otherwise bankroll the extraordinarily corrupt governments that bowed to the U.S. as we used Guatemala as a military buffer against communist infiltration of the Americas.

It's curious that Pedro's father, a manager at the banana behemoth, encouraged his family of four children to rebel against his company's chokehold on the country. It had much to do with the cultural turmoil of those times, Pedro said.

"At the end of the sixties, in my generation there were initially no radical or ideologically defined young people. We had a mix of dreams, ideals and, above all, we had an ethical or Christian commitment to the poor. Our influences were diverse and contrasted: Miguel Ángel Asturias, Cortázar, The Beatles..." In an era of rebellion driven by thumping rock and roll. The Beatles seemed the most benign influence, especially John Lennon, who was Pedro's favorite. Almost every song they sang was about love, and John's most-political lyrics challenged hot-headed young people to be careful. "You say you want a revolution"? he sang incredulously. "Well, you know, we all want to change the world. But when you talk about destruction don't you know you can count me out."

Lennon's advice: "Give peace a chance."

But Lennon was singing to students in the U.S, who enjoyed remarkable protections against violent goverment lashback when they demanded an end to the Vietnam war. In all the years of protest, the worst that happened was at Kent State, where 4 students were killed by scared citizen-soldiers. A different outcome faced protesters in Guatemala where the military was the government, Pedro said.

"The military or militarized governments of that time, fanatical in the counterinsurgency struggle and anti-communism, saw all these youthful expressions as dangerous and subversive. The oligarchs viewed with suspicion the students because, as in feudal or colonial times, they still considered them serfs.

"And then the repressive machinery began to disfigure the national territory with torture, disappearances...strafing defenseless people in stops of buses, kidnapping young people "who practiced sports suspiciously", assassinating any who dared to think and express themselves in defense of the condemned of the country."

The young had given peace its chance and, in the words of Pedro's older brother Edgar Palma Lau, decided that, "If the instrument of the enemy is violence, ours cannot be peace." The Lau brothers, like so many of their generation, had been radicalized to "take the path of armed struggle, of a war without rest and without quarter, determined to win or to die as the national anthem said." Pedro followed Edgar into the urban front, operating clandestinely within cities and towns - primarily Guatemala City, where guerrillas, although armed, acted mostly as collaborators and saboteurs, setting up safe houses where combatants could rest and where caches of arms could be stored until transported to the mountains.

As the Lau boys operated within the city, Sandra headed north to a family-owned house in Quetzaltenango, from which she worked as an armed collaborator. Her nephew, Rafael Ugarte, chuckled at the memory of being 6-years-old in the backseat of a Volkswagen while Sandra and his mother drove along the roads of Lake Atitlan, gathering food, weapons, and munitions, and putting them in the back with him. They chatted in the front seat like casual shoppers at a mall in the shadow of towering volcanoes where shadowy figures in secret camps were crafting a different kind of guerrilla organization than the three other rebel groups. ORPA's creator, Rodolfo Asturias, son of Guatemala's most famous writer, the Nobel Prize-winning Miguel Asturias, had been organizing the group quietly for eight years, developing concepts and training a mix of ladino and Mayan recruits in preparation for that day when it would make its presence publicly known. A U.S. intelligence manual described ORPA as distancing itself from the other "Marxist-Leninist" groups. "It avoided screeds about the evils of private land ownership in part because it was allying itself with the Maya people, who revered land ownership."

Sandra, Marco, and Pedro started out with ORPA as collaborators. In 1979, the year ORPA publicly declared its existence, the two men declared their allegiance and became fighters in different parts of ORPA territory. Ana, pregnant with Marcos' child, would stay underground for two more years as a collaborator, chafing at her role of stay-at-home mother. It was a breathtaking step for Pedro to drop out of college and turn his back on family, privilege, society, and the government itself, and take off the mask he had been wearing for years as an urban militant.

"I had conflicting feelings: I knew that I was going to war, to face an army experienced in the fight against guerrillas. I was 26 years old and not a beardless young man who gets into an adventure without measuring its consequences. I was perfectly aware that it was a war in which I was going to be defeated or to die, as the national anthem says, and for a guerrilla the most immediate probability is to die."

What Pedro and Marco, and eventually Sandra, did in becoming guerrillas was called "going up the mountain."

Up The Mountain

"No, Terry, you didn't go up the mountain. You went up the volcano."

My face burned at this gentle rebuke from the ex-guerrilla Tito in 2019 after I spoke of my time with the guerrillas.

"You had an adventure. We went up the mountain."

True. Even though I shared their dangers and hungers, it was for only a week and then I left and they stayed for years.

Going up the mountain was something of a holy act — a calling not everyone heard or followed; an ultimate act of choice that, if truly taken, had irrevocable consequences.

To go up the mountain was to be reborn. Many went up into the Cuchumatanes Mountains where most headline-screaming atrocities against Mayans occurred — tortures, rapes, massacres — at the hands of the army. These are the mountains I went up as a volunteer in 1972 just before the genocide, oblivious to what enraged Guatemala's young revolutionaries. Here, among these remote peaks is where the fiercest of four guerrilla groups, the EGP, took root among the trees and weavers and campesinos. Those who joined ORPA went into the volcanos of the Sierra Madres that form the country's western highlands.

To go up the mountain with ORPA was to disappear into a volcano's deepest folds...into its thickest vegetation... into places where non-humans dwelled at their wildest...where the mystical neblina fog is both blanket and one-way veil — a Harry Potter's cloak of invisibility that you learn to see out of while concealed from your pursuers, that transforms you from hunted to hunter.

"The neblina was our friend," mused Josue Sotomayor, who — as the guerrilla named Geronimo — felt his amigo's embrace for 14 cold, wet years.

To go there wasn't just a choice but a vow, and the difficult trek upwards was far less difficult than living at the destination for years, nurtured by ideals as you suffered hunger and cold and fear.

You went because once you had boiled hot.

There might have been a moment when, like the snap of a finger, you knew it was time. Previously, you had marched in protests and shook your fist and screamed your outrage. But you went home and then to class. Perhaps your eyes had burned from tear gas and maybe your skin tingled from the purple welt of a police baton. Did you know the hard pain of handcuffs? The hopeless feel of gripping jail bars? Did you weep from hearing about others being murdered, maybe a friend, son, daughter, brother, mom? Surely, you talked about these things with friends over wine. No doubt you studied your country's history and were sickened. No doubt you studied other forms of governance and were inspired. Your soul rebelled at what others suffered while you nibbled cookies and sipped strong coffee and stared without seeing.

At some point you realized that slogans and split lips and broken hearts and angry talk wouldn't bring equality any more than elections. At least not here in this stinking, corrupt system. How many Mayan babies speared by bayonets did it take to reach that conclusion? Josue didn't need something so dramatic to inspire his flight up the mountain. Bare feet were enough.

"The children had no shoes."

He repeated it to me for emphasis, but needn't have. I had lived for six months in a village of shoeless children and had traveled throughout the highlands, watching them play barefoot. It was his metaphor, a slogan, for why there was a revolution. It would have been perfect on the front of baseball caps at rallies. I can imagine it being chanted in front of the national palace by vast crowds. Who needs doctrinaire explanations from Marx or Lenin or Fidel? It's not so complicated. In one voice, the angry cry rings out:

"THEY HAVE NO SHOES"

Are you still temperate? Do you still try to see all sides, try to understand and try to make sense? Or have you turned hot, full of rage at the inequality and the savagery and the futility? At some point you might have become a collaborator, stealthily working in support of those who already were up there. Maybe you had a gun, a false name you operated under when you weren't at home eating mom's cooking. Maybe you told mom about your plans and got the reaction Tito did.

"Don't go, hijo! They will lie to you. They will lie to get you to kill for their reasons. To die for their reasons. Don't go, hijo, don't believe them. They will lie..."

But you went, anyhow, because the choice was between your mom's fears and the challenge laid down before you one day by an ORPA recruiter: are you a dreamer or a doer? A mama's boy or a man?

If you were Mayan — and used to having shit in your life — it had likely taken less to reach that point than if you were ladino. The ladino had to decide whether to accept such things and, like Ovidio, choose to work within the system or say fuck it, like Sandra and Pedro and Tito and Josue and Hernan, and go up the mountain.

It took time to reach that point of ultimate choice. To feel the flames burn down. Never had you felt so cold. Something had died within you. The old life. The old hopes and dreams. A new life awaited...

Up the mountain.

The path took you upwards to a place forged by Earth's most brutal, fiery force. You would live upon its flanks and let its hot heart re-kindle yours. The old system must be destroyed and rebuilt. The volcano, with its heritage of making something new by violently reconstructing the old, was your model, your new mother, your example of what Guatemala could be. The volcano became the symbol of ORPA, its logo, its metaphor. Its fighters were taught they were the lava of change, but first must be transformed themselves — into true believers of a cause that looked backward into their history for reasons to seek change, and forward to a future that was the change. Forward, guerrillero, to victory. *Ni un paso atras* — not one step backward. Forward or die.

A Time of War

1985

The real Ronald Reagan country was Central America

The "O" People

After coming back from Guatemala the first time, in 1973, I spent some years as a reporter in a small farm town at the foot of California's Sierra mountains. There, I licked the wounds of my pinball 20's, gave up drinking, and met a wonderful girl who sang bluegrass with her father's band at a lake where bullfrogs poked their heads out of the moss and croaked in harmony. I often fished at that lake and in my arms was the greatest catch of all. You've got it made, people told me. In an intimate moment, she whispered of wanting to get married, to have kids. "People are already calling us Mr. and Mrs. Porterville," she said - an announcement that made me realize I could no longer put off a decision that had rumbled in me for nearly two years. I yearned to move forward in my career, and Guatemala beckoned. Teletype machines at the newspaper had been spitting out stories about revolution and the massacre of Mayan people in the mountains where I had lived. My feet were itching and my heart was torn.

I decided to take a two-week solo backpack trip in the Sierra mountains to sort things out. Each day up there was wondrous, but at each sunset I started shaking with fear of bears. I knew the fear was irrational yet I still built the campfire high before entering the tent at night and pulled the sleeping bag up to my wide-open eyes. In the dancing light of shadow-flames on my tent wall, bears played and snapped their jaws, and I longed for sunrise. On the last night, I was camped among high mountain lakes above the tree line and once again huddled deep into my sleeping bag as the fire cast faces on the tent, but this time I saw people from my village — the long, smiling face of Domingo, the goofiest Mayan of them all; gaping, grinning, one-toothed Maria, the village's only beggar; drop-jawed Diego, who taught me to make adobe bricks; the village beauty, Rubidia, whose curled eyelashes were so long you could almost feel a breeze when she blinked. It seemed the whole village had come to visit, as if they were begging me to return and see what war had done to them.

The next morning, I stood on Black Rock Pass looking south over the grey granite of the Sierra, imagining that I could see as far as the Cuchumatanes Mountains of Guatemala. In that moment I decided to return as a foreign correspondent and write the story of my village, but I wasn't sure how long I would be gone, or whether I would even return.

The wonderful bluegrass singer said she would wait until waiting made no sense. "Stay in touch," she warned. We hugged goodbye and I drove out of town through fields of bent-over migrant farm workers from Mexico and Central America, and past billboards of a grinning, avuncular old dude wearing a cowboy hat next to words declaring this as "Reagan Country... Make America Great." My gut clenched....I never did like that Hollywood blow-hard...Not since I was a college journalist covering his first run for governor and saw him as a shallow slogan-slinger...So glad to finally put him behind me. I let out a whoop, gunned the accelerator, and headed south toward Guatemala — not realizing it was the real Reagan Country.

———

Little 7-year-old Angela had her arms around my neck and was giving my face kisses.

"Please don't get shot, uncle Terry," she pleaded in a sweet, tiny little voice that someday would sing opera in San Francisco.

We were in a car just over the border in Tijuana, Mexico. My older brother Lange — Angela's father — drove me here to catch a bus to Guatemala. It was cheaper than flying and I had little money. He wept inwardly, his face red and puffy as we all hugged goodbye, and I stepped into a Pullman bus with luxurious first-class seating. Jorge the driver and I quickly became friends when I caught his 3-year-old son as he flew across the aisle toward the door stairwell after Jorge threw the bus into a sharp left turn to avoid going over a steep cliff.

"Good catch, amigo," he yelled, motioning for me to come sit behind him. From then on, we chatted like hombres in the hood, as he taught me about the "O" people who often rode his bus when it headed back north to the U.S. border, and sometimes when it headed south like now.

"Amigo, these are poor people fleeing from all the danger and poverty in Guatemala, Honduras, Nicaragua, El Salvador. Even though they try to fit in and look like Mexicans, it's easy to spot them. They got these big "O" eyes that are like neon lights and their heads are always twisting around in fear. I tell them to just relax but they can't help it. At every stop, the policia get on the bus, spot the "O's" and demand money. They can't refuse or the *hijos de putas* will beat them or take the women off the bus and have their way."

He told of encounters...

A policia demanded money from a frightened mother who had only a handful of pesos left after being plucked many times since Guatemala.

"We won't be able to eat tomorrow," she cried.

He slapped her, and Jorge yelled.

"Get the fuck off my bus!"

The policia sneered.

Jorge kicked him in the balls.

Another time, when a cop threated Jorge, a man jumped up with a cocked .45 and put it at the cop's head. The policia showed his badge, the man showed his bigger federales badge. The policia whimpered and wilted and farted.

Jorge had many stories like that — of frightened, fleeing migrants and their predators. And though I had stories of my own about them from when I hitchhiked through Mexico, I stayed silent and listened and knew he was speaking truth because of what I had seen.

He said there was an "O" on this bus and challenged me to figure out who it was. It was easy, now that I knew the trick. "That woman in the third row next to the window....with owl eyes."

"Si!" laughed Jorge as he stared in his big rear-view mirror. "You'd make a good policia."

Between his unending flow of stories and wild driving, I mostly stayed awake until around midnight when we got to the border crossing at Tapachula, where my big mouth almost slammed the door shut.

"What's this?" the migration officer demanded when I opened my pack to reveal a tablet computer and printer. This was the world's first portable computer and I must have looked like some kind of spy to the bulging-eyed man sweating in tropical heat at dawn.

"My writing machine. I am a journalist," I said, producing my farm-town newspaper press pass. His eyes widened further and motioned to his superior, whose eyes also turned "O"-like as they looked at the press pass. They both puffed up to impress this obviously important person at their doorstep and started asking me questions about the revolution in Nicaragua, my political philosophy, and about my wonderful President Ronald Reagan, who has given their country so much military help in their fight against communism.

"I don't like that fucking Reagan."

He stiffened.

"You don't love your country?"

"Of course I do, but in my country we are free men, free to disagree with our president. Are you not free men here?"

Ahhh, shit, his eyes were suddenly cocked and his left hand reached toward the passport he had just stamped.

"Hurry! Hurry!" the bus driver yelled as he suddenly entered the office. "The bus is leaving." He grabbed my backpack and threw it, straps and buckles flailing, atop the bus.

"Later," I yelled at the officer, snatching the passport and rushing away with a curse in my throat.

Start shutting the fuck up, Terry.

It was my first, tiny taste of what lay before me in this tension-gripped land that didn't feel quite the same as I got on the bus and in the midst of looking for something to make me smile, fell asleep until the rumble of paving stones awoke me hours later in Antigua, the ancient Spanish colonial capital of Guatemala established in 1543 by Spanish conquistadors. After a few weeks of Spanish language study, I hopped on a different kind of bus that would take me back to my village of Cunén. It was no Pullman. It was a "chicken bus".

The Chicken Bus

Death traps is what I call these diesel-stinking, smoke-belching, horn-blasting, color-drenched contraptions that still prowl the streets of Guatemala villages and towns. They are school buses banned from the United States because they are too dangerous for our kids, but not for theirs. It's how lower-income Guatemalans get around. They are officially called chicken buses because of all the chickens and other critters people drag aboard — pigs and goats and sheep and Christ knows what. They look like flocks of parrots as they cruise the streets, competing for riders with a driver's assistant hanging out with one hand and snatching passengers with the other. The bus's foreheads are stamped with their ultimate destination such as Xela or Quiche or Panajachel or...

"Cunén?"

"Si, Senor, come aboard."

The fare was 4 quetzales. I handed the driver a 5-quetzal bill — about a dollar — but instead of giving me change, the driver held it aloft. He was classic, this guy, with his swollen belly and sweaty, smiling, hairy face full of mischief.

"Second class, senor?"

He nodded at all the humanity stuffed onto bench seats with boards stretched between them so that eight — or even ten people if some are kids — could sit mushed together with their creatures and tortillas and bags of clothing or wheat or maize or vegetables crammed in among them.

Or, he wiggled the bill, "First class?"

He nodded toward his assistant, far to the rear, who was holding open a precious clear space in the middle of the back seat.

"Keep the change."

It was a long, funky scramble through and over the people and their belongings, but they were small and I am tall so it was not hard so much as it was an adventure, stepping on bags that writhed and wriggled and made odd noises as my seven-league legs took me hovering over upturned faces that grinned at my crotch passing overhead, and I swear if they weren't so quiet by nature that the whole bus would have shaken with laughter by the time I finally reached first-class and sat down.

This is what that first-class ticket bought.

On my right was the soft hip of a weary, thin-faced Mayan woman - she was from Nebaj! I could tell by her trademark red corte (dress) with vertical dotted lines and her huipile (blouse) intricately interwoven with a mix of colorful geometric designs and creatures. A long, thick twisted rainbow ribbon with fuzzy cotton balls enwrapped the top of her head — weaving in and out of her matted greying hair until it rose as something of an edifice. I knew it was the weight of her world not the archictecture that made her head droop.

On my left was the hard hip of an ancient-looking Mayan farmer. His brown face was as deeply furrowed as a corn row and his broad nose drooled thick strings of white goo that shot out when he coughed deep from his lungs. Whatever was firing off those lethal discharges would get me eventually and slowly take me down.

My feet came to rest on gunny sacks full of squealing piglets who constantly moved, making my knees plunge up and down like the pistons of the bus engine you could hear all the way back here in first-class. And then, with a long blast of the air horn and a black gush of exhaust smoke — amid clucking, crowing, squealing, and coughing — we were off to the land of Maya and of faces, I prayed, who were still living and might just brighten when they saw mine again.

It was a long journey of starts and stops at every town or village or wide spot where someone with an upraised hand stood to be picked up, but slowly we crawled out of the hustle of city-type settlements upwards into hills that gave birth to mountains that are the heartland of people I sought. We chugged up slopes blanketed with rows of towering, green corn stalks that fought the winds of gravity, trying to stay erect as the land steepened so much that farmers sometime fell from their fields, breaking bones. Small, dark dots moved among them — men, boys, and girls with hoes and baskets, harvesting what's ripe and beating back weeds, bushes, and vines invading from the forest edges. Mama, and maybe her mama, too, was at home with children too big to carry into the fields and too small to work. They crush the corn with stone rollers until it is mushy. Then they form it into fist-size balls to be slapped flat as tortillas, which is what they are. Their homes, built upon level patches scraped out of the slopes or atop hillocks, were made of mud-plastered sticks or of adobe bricks. Some were whitewashed. Most were roofed over with fronds — free for the taking — but a very few had roofs of expensive tile or shiny sheets of corrugated metal called lamina. As we were far from the hurricane zone but right in the middle of earthquake central, I thought I might choose the poorer family's fronded home over the pricey tile-roofed adobe. I mean, what would you rather have fall on your head in a hard shake?

Funny what goes through one's head when its owner is anticipating his heart's destination. Cunén's slopes look so much like these. As do its people....Domingo, Maria, Diego....

Now we were dropping into a river valley before climbing the great Cuchumatanes mountain range where Cunén dwells. How well I remember the sparkling little village, Sacapulas, along the green waters of the Chixoy River.

Green? I remembered it as blue. A newspaper colleague remembered it as tragic. Her boyfriend drowned in it while kayaking. There was a new bridge replacing the fallen one that had forced buses in 1972 to ford the river as we passengers clutched invisible rosaries and whispered long-misplaced prayers of benediction while the bus shivered in forceful current. Scary stuff then but maybe not as stressful as what awaited us on the other end of the new bridge — a machine-gun guard post where every vehicle stopped and every passenger got out to be inspected and interrogated by gun-flashing soldiers.

An old woman sold me a slice of watermelon for five centavos. I gave her 50 and she flashed a smile big as that slice.

Then, back on the bus I leaped as it started its harshest labor, grinding up the steepest road of the journey to that ridge top high above where I had run in the moonlight 12 years before, grinning. I was grinning again as we ate the altitude. Almost there. Almost there.

"Papeles, señor."

The ridge-top guard station was no more than a skinny log stretched across two rocks where patrulleros — civilians forced to act like soldiers and armed with a firearm or, most often, machete — sat until a vehicle happened by for a shakedown. A blue-and-white national flag fluttered from a pole made of a tree limb. The poor, ignorant fellow who wanted to see my papers couldn't read them, but no matter, what he really wanted was coin. ""Un quetzal," he demanded, withholding my passport with one hand behind his back while holding palm-up his permanently dirty and thickly calloused right hand. I gave him 50 centavos and he waved us on with the same slice of a smile the watermelon woman gave me.

The skinny, gnarled, arm-severed old pine tree was still where I remembered, at the point where the ridge road starts diving down to my village. "Alto!" I yelled to the driver. He and his assistant, the only other people still on the bus, turned to look at me. "Momento," I pleaded and clambered to the top of the bus for a better view of... Cunén.

It looked as magical to me as Nebaj did when first I laid eyes on it — nestled in a small plain at the foot of two descending mountains and a hill. Late afternoon shadows soon would quench the glow of its vast, whitewashed cemetery and the humbler white dot of its old church. Sparkles bounced off metal roofs. Hidden by the toe of that nearest mountain was the upward sprawling valley of Los Trigales, the village's patchwork treasure trove of wheat fields. Soon, my fluttering insides told me, we'll be there!

"Vamonos!" I cried after leaping back into the bus.

No holding back this energized driver, who unloosed the hand brake and goosed the accelerator. Down we rumbled as I glued my nose to the window and looked for sweet memories. First, was the blown-out piece of mountain side visible to all in Cunén when they look up. The faithful say it is where the Virgin of Candelaria appeared with her warning for the village maidens to stay pure or else, or at least that's what the drunken Domingo told me, and that's what I told a young American named Mary who refused to walk past that point for fear of rocks falling as penance upon her, and that's what a visiting anthropologist wrote down when I told her the story, and that's what went into her serious and sober report about this ancient village and the road that Spanish Conquistadors came down on horses, the road we were banging along no faster than they did. We only slowed once, for the big zig switchback, and sped up for the steep, final descent into the valley.

The road leveled off after a swooping right turn that brought us at eye-level with tall rows of green corn on the right and squares of golden wheat to the left. Rutted and rocky, the road merrily bounced us about as I waved to campesino men dressed in white, calf-length pants, carrying wood stacked on their hunched-over backs.

I stuck my happy, dog head out the window.

"Hola!" I yelled to them.

"Hola," they replied with surprise in their quieter voices.

Hola to every man, woman, child and fleeing cur as our bus reached the creek crossing and gathered power for the final uphill spurt through adobe and brick single-story buildings — some whitewashed, some painted in blues and pinks and yellows, all with open windows facing the road, most with faces gawking out for this rare diversion. Hola, hola, hola, we yelled at each other as the bus banged and roared and swayed on its aching springs until we turned right into the village square across from the church and the driver pulled on his air horn, hit the brakes, and skidded to a stop. Almost bursting with joy, I stepped back into the world of Cunèn as the bus rattled off.

A Killing

Alone.

Where is everybody?

There was always someone in the village square, night or day. Crowds, usually, but now no one, not even old Diego who had neverendingly swept the church steps. Alone, until some patojos, slang for boys, emerged from hiding among the buildings and gathered around me, gawking up at perhaps the tallest person they had ever seen. I gazed back, trying to connect.

Who will throw the first stone?

It happened in every village I walked through before. The boys would come jabbering towards me and one — the bravest — would rock me as a sign of leadership. *Come on, boys,* I thought with an odd sense of yearning. *Throw me a welcome.*

Not a pebble.

Suddenly, a middle-aged ladino man came round the corner and shuffled toward me while raising his left hand to his cheek. He was tall for this village — perhaps 5'9" — and separated into two bulges by a straining leather belt. Underneath the perspiration of effort and the redness of consternation, his mildly handsome, lightly whiskered face was pale. He wore a turtleneck sweater the color of dust, and curly black hair crowded his head. Ten steps away, he stopped, stared at me, squeezed folds of cheek skin, thrust his right arm upwards, and cried out.

"AIEEEEEE!"

I froze.

"How sad what has happened, so very sad," the man wept in sorrowful, high-pitched Spanish as he shuffled toward me while offering his right hand to shake mine and introducing himself as Hector, the poet of Cunèn.

"What is sad?" I asked as my shaky fingers grasped his soft ones.

The top bulge expanded with a deep, sucking breath and sagged over his belt as he exhaled the answer.

"There was a killing."

Just the day before, a soldier leveled his rifle at a young Mayan boy standing on the church steps. The M-1 was a gift from the United States to the Guatemalan Army, which was fighting international communism on our behalf in villages like Cunèn.

"He wasn't just any boy. He was the *gran patojo*," Hector said — the best boy in the village...only 14...the son of a campesino who had worked all his life like a dog, nay, a pack of dogs, in his steep rocky farmland, going without, making his family go without so he could save enough money to send his boy away to become a priest. He represented hope, not just for the family but for the village, and his story resonated with me: *I was 14 when my parents made the big sacrifice of sending me to the seminary.*

The patojos

The soldier aimed his rifle as he spat out hate.

"I am going to kill you."

The boy, Juan Botón, said nothing.

The bullet went straight through his chest.

Just an idiot with power in his hands and contempt within, Hector said. He was Mayan like the boy he shot, conscripted into the Army and taught to think of his own people as dumb Indian shit infected by the communism of guerrillas living among surrounding mountains. Army recruits, some 15 some 50, were drafted on Sundays when villagers gathered in the town square after church, many of them young men flirting with young women who had come for the same reason. There was no notice like I got when the U.S. army tried to draft me; soldiers just showed up in trucks, surrounded the square, and grabbed every man who could walk. In my previous time here, I watched as they conducted a fitness test by leading them into a nearby single-story structure and ordering them to jump out of the window. If you didn't break a leg, you were shoved into the bed of a stake truck and driven off to boot camp.

I wonder if the boy's killer had been drafted in this town square?

"Come," Hector said, tugging me by my left wrist from the spot I had frozen in. "You can stay with me."

He walked one stolid step after another in beat-up brown shoes, which helped identify him as a ladino. Mayans usually wore sandals or went barefoot. Being a ladino in Guatemala, then, was like being white in the U.S. It didn't grant you success but it opened the door to opportunity even if you do start as the janitor. It was understood by all that If you want to get ahead in Guatemala, take off the sandals and put on some shoes. Get rid of those hand-woven clothes and put on some store-bought. Learn Spanish. Hop on a chicken bus to Guatemala City. Live like a cockroach in the city's seams and cracks and frayed edges. Pray for success as you dodge drugs and gangs and disease, or flee to the U.S. border. If nothing works, go home, pick up your hoe and try to dig a future for your children. Good luck.

"Hola, don Paco," two barefoot native women said softly to Hector as we walked by an adobe building on the corner. It looked familiar.

"Say, Hector, this used to be the mayor's store. His daughter stood outside of it all day, always dressed like she was going to a dance, with curled eye lashes and lots of makeup. She looked with those yearning, advertising eyes at every car and bus that came into town."

"Rubidia!" He tilted his head back, rolled his puppy eyes, and spoke of how she had captured the heart of a wealthy Mexican man, married, moved to the United States, and, presumably, lived happlily ever after.

"What about Elvia?" She was Rubidia's main rival. Elvia had been the captain of the girls' basketball team I coached. Aggressive. Always went for the ball. Didn't stand around waiting for it. All spunk, no lipstick.

"After Rubidia left, Elvia went to Guatemala City and found a job in the airport clothing store."

She, too, escaped, but I wondered, did she really?

People who left villages like Cunén, seeking a better life, often ended up in the even-worse poverty of Guatemala City's fringes. Morse once took me to visit living quarters made out of cardboard and rotted plywood and bits of lumber and metal. Individuals and families lived in rooms sealed with rags stuffed into the seams to keep out the cold and plastic over the rags to keep out the rain. Walls were shared. Family after family. Room after room for an entire block. It was said you could push on one end of that block and see the room at the other end move. The communal toilet flowed down the middle of the dirt road into a canyon stream choked with toilet paper and every other kind of trash.

But it was worse at the city dump, called a *basurero*.

This was a third-world basurero and what flowed out of its dump trucks looked like a stew of sludge — rotted, rusted, congealed stuff glued together by decomposing food slime. Plastic bags fluttered out when the truck tilted up to let it all flush out. Vultures hopped around, digging in the slime with their beaks, competing with entire Mayan families who lived there amid the garbage. In their villages they would be working the fields. Here, mom and dad and sister and brother harvested the trucks for scraps of poverty garbage they shoved into burlap sacks that dragged on the ground, reminding me of black sharecroppers working cotton fields I saw as a child in Kentucky.

But most people just stayed in their villages. Hector was one of those.

"I will never leave. I will die here....perhaps soon," Hector said as we strolled the road to his house. He talked, walked, and acted sad. He was 50. His father was 53 when he died. His brother was 53 when he died. Hector had heart problems. There were no doctors. "Soon I will die and they will take me to the cemetery and cover me with whitewash," he sighed.

"Hola, don Paco." Two little ladino girls in school uniforms stopped running as we walked past them, stared at me, and then skipped off. They wore shoes.

Hector lived in a simple, concrete block, two-room dwelling some doors down. It had a small courtyard with a wooden door to the street. He let me cast down my sleeping bag on a couch in the front room.

"Casa Ayuda, where I lived before, is just across the street."

Hector snorted. "The 'great' Raul Castillo was born there." Castillo was the country's ambassador to the United Nations. I had met him the year before while I was a journalist covering the world's first conference on environment in Sweden. There, he sought my attention and treated me with respect, but here he treated me as an inferior, I told Hector, whose face darkened.

"Not one quetzal, not one centavo has the great man given to his pueblo. Not during the earthquakes, not during the famines, not during the war, not to our little clinic. Nothing!" His head rolled back and forth atop flesh squeezed up from the collar of his turtleneck. "Oh, Terry, we miss Ayuda." All the volunteers left two years before when the Army and guerrillas clashed in the mountains above Cunén where Nebaj is. "Ay, Dios, it was terrible."

He knew of massacres up there, but here in Cunén only 10 died when half-a-dozen guerrillas snuck down the mountainside one day to attack symbols of the ruling class. They shot up the town center, killed some police and town functionaries, chased the mayor out the back door of his house up into the hills where he hid out, and blew up city hall. Then they stole a car and went back up the mountain.

"That was the end of our war. Cunén is very lucky."

But, ay Dios, the volunteers never came back — one of the unwritten tragedies of the war. Dorotea the healer, Morse the builder. Volunteers like them fled back to the United States when the Army flooded the highlands with commie-killing soldiers in the early 1980's. Anyone was considered a 'commie' who gave the people hope, who educated them about opportunity, who whispered into their ears about heritage lost and heritage that might be theirs again. It didn't matter whether it was a teacher with chalk in a classroom or a teacher with a gun in the forest or a priest with an idea to create cooperatives. All were suspect. Many were killed. Many fled north in what was the first flood of migrants toward the U.S. border.

Don Paco took me to the locked gate of Casa Ayuda and pounded on it. No answer.

"Do you see? No one is at home."

Next to it was the school I helped build with mud and cement and more hard work than I ever did before or since. The teachers were long gone, but not the memory of Morse, who met me in September 1972 when I stepped off a chicken bus during my first trip to Cunén. He was the lead volunteer of a group called Ayuda (help in Spanish) I learned about one hungover morning in a Southern California coffee shop where I sat across from an older woman who had been a volunteer in Cunén. I was mourning a major life rejection. "Me!" I cried, who had won national awards for my work with The Tuberculosis Association. As I finished on a weepy note, she reached across the table, took my hands gently as the kindly Red Cross nurse had years before, and said words that, like the nurse's, changed the course of my life...*The people are poor and hungry and dying of tuberculosis...All you have is a broken heart...Heal them and heal yourself.* Three weeks later, hefting a backpack full of tuberculosis medicines, I got off that chicken bus and met the toughest man I've ever known.

The Toughest Man

"Are you Terry? Get your stuff and follow me."

His steps were sure and balanced. Steady. Straightforward. Strong. Morse, I soon discovered, was as he appeared.

I hoisted my new, blue backpack and stumbled behind him to the high, white adobe walls of "Casa Ayuda" as he called it, and walked through the wooden gate into an open, grassy courtyard surrounded by doors that led to rooms. He took me to a large room with several wooden bed platforms in it. "You'll sleep here," he said pointing to a platform. I tossed down the pack. He ordered me to pick it up and place it on the bed.

Morse was one of two permanent volunteers. He was not much bigger than the Mayan men but smaller than stoutish Dorothy, the nurse who ran the clinic with no-nonsense care and often threw her arms up, jazz-handing the air as she prayed for God's blessing upon incurably ill people. Morse ran the agricultural and building programs with soft, terse commands that stabbed out of his half-smiling lips like the thrust of a bayonet, and sized people up with a glance. Like me for instance. When I told him I was here to start an anti-TB program, his eyes x-rayed me from my tennis shoes to my shaggy, long hair.

"Come with me."

We went out to the grassy area where he reached down and picked up a machete.

"You came to cure tuberculosis?"

"Yeah, well..."

"Let's start by cutting the grass."

Morse handed me the machete, told me how to use it, told me to get down on my knees, and left.

I spent that first day, a Monday, learning how not to be killed by an instrument made from the steel spring of an old truck. The machete springs back if you hit the ground with it at the wrong angle. I dodged the guillotine blade numerous times before I got the knack, all the while remembering how I hated using my dad's lawn mower to cut our lawns — hated it so much that I vowed never to have a lawn of my own. And haven't. Nor a mower. Nor a machete.

On Tuesday, Morse taught me how to mix concrete with a shovel in a constant mixing rhythm. The thing is, you can't stop or the mixture will get hot and set like a rock in that wheelbarrow. Morse threw in cement, water and gravel; another volunteer and I turned the mixture over and over, hour by hour. Can't stop except when Morse tips the wheelbarrow into the area where he and Diego were making the slab for our school. Hours of pain streaked through every nerve path of my back and arms. At noon we took a lunch break, but I went straight to my cot and flopped down with an exhale of gratitude.

"Get those muddy boots off that blanket!"

Morse stared down at me.

"You're dirtying a blanket that someone who is not you washed by hand."

Shame flushed the pain out of me.

"Let's go!"

He dragged me off for an afternoon of the same. At dawn he was back.

On Thursday, he gave me to the old man Diego, whose mouth held two precious teeth, to learn the craft of making adobe bricks. I thought Diego was the planet's happiest dude with his perpetual gaping smile, but soon realized he had a malady that let his jaw droop like that of a grinning dead man. The few words he spoke came more from his throat than from his lips, but he chuckled a lot and made a good audience and was a good adobe teacher. He also swept the church steps with a witch's broom of corn straw bound to a thin branch.

I couldn't move on Friday, so I ignored Morse's cryptic commands and spent all day tied up in cramps while watching a family of mice play next to me on the concrete floor.

After about two weeks of this, I rebelled.

"Look, Morse, I didn't come here to mix mud. It's time to start that anti-TB program."

Dorothy, who by this time had seen too many Indians planted in the cemetery because of TB, agreed.

Morse drove me down to Guatemala City, where there was a huge hospital filled with hundreds of TB patients. That's how they treated TB in those days — by keeping the sick from infecting the healthy. In the U.S., we were shutting down TB warehouses because our standard of living plus antibiotics wiped it out. That's what Guatemalans needed — a better life. Instead, they got me.

I boldly knocked upon the hospital doors and introduced myself in remarkably bad Spanish as a former member of the TB Association, the original name of the Lung Association, here to develop a program in Cunèn. I was immediately ushered into the radiology department where a doctor in a white coat stood before lung x-rays pinned against a light table on the wall. He addressed me respectfully in Spanish.

"Dr. Winckler, I am so glad you came. I am troubled by what I see on these xrays and need your advice." He pointed to a smudge on a lung.

Gulp. You fucked this up, Winckler. He thinks you are a doctor.

It took some red-faced stammering and finally an English-speaking nurse to clear up the mistake. She helped me explain my real mission and to create a plan. They would gladly train someone from our village in basic prevention and treatment of TB, and would provide said person with supplies to get him started. It would take about three months of training. The person could stay in the hotel across the street. All we had to do was pay for the housing and food costs.

Deal!

Morse was so thrilled at our plan that he took me climbing that afternoon on Fuego, an occasionally furious volcano that killed hundreds when it exploded in 2018. Fuego wasn't spurting lava when Morse led me up its blackened flanks — just hissing from holes in its sides. Every few minutes it bellowed out a blast of steam and rocks. Morse urged me up its warm, shifty sands to a cone lip of thick, yellow sulphuric rock.

"Don't be afraid, Terry. Come here and look."

Fumes stung my eyes and nose. The cone trembled. It was ready for a blow.

"Just clearing its sinuses," Morse said, pulling me by the hand to stand upon a yellow crunchy, precipice and look straight into the throat of hell. Lava and steam bubbled, rocks streamed down from the inner core, coating the gurgling mass like a dessert topping of grey melted sugar. The cone shook harder and the lava mess sucked in.

"Step back, Terry, it's going to burp."

We did just before it did with a roaring punch of air that spat stones and steam just above our heads.

"Like a howitzer," Morse muttered, providing another clue to his past.

We skied back down the black sands on our shoe soles, whooping like kids. It was such a great day for Morse and I for we had accomplished our public health mission and earned the right to play. We laughed and reminisced all the way back to Cunèn where Dorothy reacted to the news with a shouted, "Thank you, Lord!" She knew just who we should pick for the training — a 19-year-old boy named Carlos who live in Chicaman, a village just south of Cunén.

Carlos' parents were even more thrilled than Dorothy. Their son had a chance to break out, to escape up a ladder invisible to most Mayans. He would go to the big city, to be trained as a doctor! Not exactly, we explained, but to them it was just the first step. Soon, they imagined, he would get more training to become a healer with a white coat. He would become renown among his people and live the good life and help bring the good life to his family and village.

We all became infected with their joy and that helped us raise money for Carlos' expenses. His parents chipped in, we chipped in, and as the word spread — "Carlos is becoming a doctor!" — people from among the aldeas (hamlets) and village chipped in. We had an abundace of funding, enough even for new clothes, and soon it was time to drive Carlos to the city. The trip began ominously when a Mayan boy with a burst appendix came into Dorothy's clinic as we were getting to leave and she implored us to take him to the closest hospital in Quiche on our way. "Drive fast, he may die!"

I drove that rusty yellow pickup truck as if the tight windy mountain roads were mine alone...flinging gravel on other vehicles we ripped past, making people with their heavy burdens scatter. Morse, who rarely showed emotion, prayed in bursts.

"God... God...God."

The boy still lived 50 miles later when we screeched up to the hospital and raced him in. Then we took off at a leisurely pace, Morse and I and the pale-faced Carlos, laughing at some of the close calls. Soon we were dropping Carlos off at the hotel across the street from the TB hospital. Kindly women smiled at us from open doors as we walked to Carlos' room. The kid was a little scared. Hell, he had never left his village before, let alone come to a fast-paced, traffic-choked city, let alone spend a night in a room alone with sheets, and awaken to food in abundant quantity and variety. All so wonderfully overwhelming.

We assured Carlos that things would be great and quickly left, lest the boy leap into our truck and refuse to stay. All the way home, Morse and I congratulated ourselves on a job well done, and once again Dorothy threw her hands in the air and thanked God. And I slept well until the sun rose.

"Get up, Terry, it's time to work."

New dawn, new day, same old Morse. He introduced me to Domingo. Lots of teeth, lots of grinning, lots of nose with the swollen look of lots of alcohol. Me and Domingo became instant best buds.

Domingo took me out into the demonstration field of wheat Ayuda was growing with the aid of chemical fertilizer next to a campesino's field. Astounding difference. Twice as tall and more thickly laden with grain. You have to demonstrate new things to these people who dare not experiment with so much at stake if things go wrong. No wonder I was so constantly stopped on the streets by farmers begging me for 'quimico bueno' - the good chemical.

Domingo demonstrated how to cut the miracle wheat, using a wicked hand sickle so sharp it scared me looking at the blade. The method is, bend over until your back hurts, pull together a handful of the stalks and saw at them until they are cut through. Tie the stalks in a bundle, throw on the ground and repeat.

Fifteen minutes into the backbending, I thought that Domingo wasn't progressive enough in his technique — that a blade so sharp should be used to chop like the wheat cutter did in that famous painting, "The Reaper," with a large scythe.

"*Mire*, Domingo," I said, calling him over for a demonstration.

I grabbed a bunch of stalks.

"Si."

And twisted them as he had shown.

"Si."

And took a mightly swing at them as the painting showed. The sickle caromed off the stalks into my palm, cutting a neat, blood-squirting half-moon.

"Si."

Dorothy squirted novocaine into the wound and stitched it with big overhand knots that left a lifelong, lumpy scar.

"Back to work," Dorothy said after cinching the last knot.

Domingo seemed extra goofy when I came back and showed him.

"Cusha?" he asked, lifting his right thumb to his lips in a well-rehearsed imitation of someone drinking a pint bottle of the local moonshine.

Morse was coming. I shook my head.

"Pues, tonight then. There is a party up in Los Trigales."

Morse hurried us along.

"The day isn't forever. That wheat needs threshing and winnowing while the wind still blows."

Domingo started stuffing wheat bundles into a circular net bag made by hand of twisted hemp. The bag expands as bundles go in. At about five feet feet in diameter, two-feet thick, and heavy as an adobe slab-brick, it's full. An old Mayan man half an inch taller than the bag took it upon his back in one twisting feat and trotted toward Domingo's house a quarter a mile away. All you could see of him were the tire treads of his sandals.

"Let me," I said after Domingo stuffed another sack.

I reached down, grasped the net bag, poured strength into my thin arms, used the same twisting yank and fell on it with an oof.

"Here," said Domingo, easily lifting it up off the ground. I turned and he placed it upon my back as I grasped its edges. Heavy like the weight of the world. *God how do these people so much smaller than me do it?* The answer is, they have no choice. I staggered along, determined not to drop it in front of men who measure you by the burdens you carry.

There was a flat clay mud area outside his house where the other bag had been placed. At Domingo's direction, we spread both bags' wheat in a circle about 12 feet across. He lashed two horses together side by side and guided them around the wheat as their hooves smashed down, dislodging the kernels from the chaff. Inevitably, the horses dropped steaming hunks of manure in the wheat. Without slowing down, Doming snatched the hunks one by one and slung them to the side. The last hunk he held to his grinning lips.

"Pan dulce!" Sweet bread. He pretended to take a big bite, then paused, looked at me with a wicked grin and said he was thirsty.

"Cusha?"

For the only time in Cunén, I got drunk that night, in a small adobe building with a red tile roof atop a mesa high up in Los Trigales. The place was so stuffed with Mayan men and women that the marimba band could hardly play. Everybody got drunk on clear, vile cusha moonshine and swayed as one because we were all so packed together. No one could fall down, even if they were passed out or dead. Your body would just keep dancing.

Morse was not happy at dawn the next morning as he shook me violently awake, then took me on a walk up the road to town central so I could see all the Mayan bodies — whole families — drunk along the road and sidewalks.

"They have an excuse. Their lives are harsh. Their choices are few."

He worked me hard that day, worked me through lunch, worked me all afternoon without respite, and sweated the cusha out of me. A few days later, Morse told me to quit working and come with him to the clinic.

"We got a problem."

Carlos was back after less than three weeks. He was supposed to stay twelve. Morse and I entered the clinic to see him sitting on the clinic's examination table as Dorothy finished shooting something into his arm with a hypodermic needle. His face was turned so much away from us that we could only see a left ear poking out from all the black hair, but Dorothy's angry face turned toward us.

"You fools put him in a hotel full of prostitutes! A 19-year-old boy who had never touched a woman. A kid with more money than he or anybody in that hotel had ever seen before."

Carlos had spent every night and every centavo in a different hotel room, picking up a severe case of venereal disease in the process. About the only thing he learned at the hospital was how to inject himself with penicillin — but, damn, what a way to get sick!

Dorothy seethed at us, not Carlos, and sent him home

to Chicaman after sending us back to the compound with a serious tongue-lashing. It was the only time I felt Morse and I were equals, though it didn't last. The next morning, Morse shook me awake.

"The sun is shining."

A Song In My Heart

A few weeks later, needing a break from Morse, I took that bus ride to Nebaj and ran back to Cunén to finish building the school. We finished within a couple of months, giving Mayan kids an eye-opening chance to see a way out of these difficult fields, and that's when it struck me: what's the path out of poverty when kids from Cunén get their eyes opened by schooling? Where's their ladder up in a society where skin color is the first rung? For a white-skinned *Norteamericano* like me, lots of ladders awaited just 2,500 miles away, even though I had no airline ticket, only $10, little common sense, but an abundance of can-do attitude, and a song in my heart that came pouring out as I began my journey home with a 50-mile walk to Huehuetenango. I paused atop the high road overlooking my little village and tearfully gazed goodbye, then spun about and walked down the steep dirt road on the other side as verses of the first song I ever composed came out of me step-by-step. Inspired by the melodious-sounding destination —*way-way-ten-ango* —I sang out with a special joy that returns every time I sing it:

It's a long way, a tough way,
A gritty, grinding, rough way,

A mean way, a hot way,
A slithery mountainous way-ay
All the way to Huehuetenango
And the road is fer-de-lance in your legs,
And the sun dios del fuego,
And you curse this day, this goddamned day,
On the way to Huehuetenago
At Aquacatan, 10 kilos more, I paused to drink un poco,
The Indian folk asked, "Donde vas?"
Huehue, I cried!
Huehue? By foot?
"MUY LOCO!"

And so the song and my legs continued in rhythm until, at the very edge of Huehue, a hippie couple in a VW camper van pulled up, told me to get the hell in, and off we went — the first of several rides ending at Tapachula, a Mexican border town where caravans of today's migrants pass through, but only a sprinkling back then. I crossed over with a mouth full of melody and a white-skin passport that encouraged truck drivers to pick me up as dark-skinned others watched, knowing they would never get a free ride. I suspect they walked much further than my 50 miles and without a song in their hearts. What I didn't know —how could I have? — is that a Catholic priest named Father Greg was resting his aching feet in Guatemala at the base of Volcano Toliman after just walking *3,000 miles from Minnesota through Mexico* along the same migrant route I was on. Unlike me, he hadn't shrugged his shoulders at the impossibility of poverty but plunged into the problem like a running back with a dream cradled in his arms, raising money from donors around the world with every step he took. Like Ana, he never took one step back as he headed toward the same volcanoes she would some day, and for the same reason: to revolutionize Mayan lives with the radical idea that inspired the revolution — land for Mayans. In 12 years, our lives will intertwine at those volcanoes, but now my outstretched thumb was taking me in an opposite direction.

Thirty hours and several truck rides after leaving Tapachula, I was in Guadalajara, wondering which way leads home. I hoisted the blue backpack, shrugged it onto my shoulders, snapped the belt buckle, and looked around. It was near midnight on the edge of a plaza, encircled by a road, and I was alone, except for bugs clattering against the yellow street lamp above my head. A fountain gently splashed somewhere in the gloom. Without any sense of direction, I started walking thataway.

It was a short walk.

"Yoo hoo, gringo, are you hungry?"

A taxi was keeping pace with me a few feet away, and out of its rear window hung two, beautiful, jiggling breasts.

I laughed. So did the woman's ruby lips.

"No gracias, señorita."

The taxi took off and disappeared around the plaza as I strode with lighter steps and a mouth full of grin.

"Come close, gringo, have a taste."

They were back and she was shaking them like maracas.

Oh how hungry I was. Not for nippled loaves but for street tacos — al pastor! — or even the scrap of a tortilla fallen on the street that dogs would fight over. That I would fight the dogs for.

"Not tonight, querida."

The taxi took off for another circle of the plaza, joined by two others who fell in behind it, flashing their lights and honking. A parade of prostitutes? I leaned into the straps of my pack and hot-legged across the street to a cemetery surrounded by a high brick wall and flattened myself against it with my arms stretched out, trying to blend in with the bricks. Slowly, I sidestepped until the honking and cries of "Gringo..." faded and the only sound was of whiskered cheek on rough concrete as I inched along like a crab fleeing the tentacles of a hungry octopus.

My left fingertips touched cold metal that instantly began snarling and shaking — a gate of twisted iron rods seized in the fangs of a demonic black dog trying to bite through at me. I jerked away, more mesmerized than afraid, as drool drizzled down the bars.

Suddenly, a soft whistle and the dog vanished without taking my fear with him.

What's that moving toward me? It's floating, isn't it? A ghost?

A vague figure appeared from among the headstones with bright eyes peering through the fence rods at my gaunt, tousle-haired, frightened self. He nodded, dug into his pocket, and produced something at eye level between his thumb and forefinger that glowed yellow as a harvest moon in the incandescence of street lamps and glinted as he turned it back and forth.

"Do you know pesos, señor?"

"Pesos?"

With the thunk of a thumbnail, the golden object tumbled over the fence into my cupped palms where, shielded from the street light, it turned silver, and though my Spanish was poor even I knew what the embossed word *CIEN* meant. One hundred pesos! Nearly five dollars. I could eat extravagantly for a day or humbly for three.

He was gone when I looked up, but his voice floated from the other side.

"Give it away when you aren't hungry."

I wrapped my right fist around the coin, thrust it into my pocket and turned it over and over and over in my mind as I returned to the sidewalk at a ponderer's pace, following a wall that pointed like a compass needle into the night.

"Señor."

A sleek, long, glistening black car had stopped along the curb next to me, its driver stretched across the front seat and looking up with his pale face through the passenger window.

"Señor gringo, please let me give you a ride."

One must always ride the lucky wave.

I opened the door, threw my pack into the back seat and slid in the front seat.

The driver started sobbing.

"I am so lonely and unhappy. Will you have dinner with me tonight? I need a friend. I will pay. Please, señor gringo."

"My name is Terry. Of course."

Lubricated by tears and alcohol, his story flowed out. He was an attorney - and homosexual in a society that scorned *maricons*, a word Latin men spat out like a bullet in those days, and many still do. At times it became too much so he would get into his sleek vehicle to drive the sadness away.

"I know you are not a maricon, señor Terrry." He trilled the r's in my name as Latin people love to do when they say it. "I know these things, but just be my friend this night."

He kept talking as we ate steak in a posh restaurant. He was a rich, handsome man with slicked-back black hair and wrinkle-free skin in which pathos surged, and he hated himself for being gay — the first openly gay man I had ever spent time with — but the strangeness disappeared with the chewing of delicious meat, and we smiled at each other as the homophobia I had been raised with began dissolving. The story continued through dessert, many cups of coffee, and a ride to the outskirts of Guadalajara where the now-sober attorney begged me to stay in his car and keep talking.

"I will drive you home, señor Terrry."

I didn't have enough story left for a 1,200-mile drive.

"You are too kind and I am so grateful for being such a friend to this stranger," I said while getting out at a truck stop where a dozen or so migrants waited for rides. He drove away as I stuck my thumb out and almost instantly got a ride, leaving the others behind as the truck driver drove me 300 miles to Mazatlan, offering to share his lunch, which I declined while patting my full belly. I stepped off the truck amid more migrants, who were stoically enduring rough treatment by state and federal policia, especially women whose various parts were patted or squeezed by badge-wearers looking for, uh, weapons or contraband. Man or woman, they all wore "O" eyes I will never forget and I wondered, while stepping across the U.S. border a week later, if their hard journey had earned them a chance at opportunities that instantly were mine in abundance. It's a question I thought about for 12 years until I returned to Cunèn and saw the village's best boy dead at the foot of a ladder built by his father one hoe-chop at a time over many years.

In 1973, the author hitchhiked through Mexico from Guatemala along the migrant route

July 1, 1985 - "My Bones!"

Clanging church bells awoke me the morning after my return to Cunén, and I went out to see little dots moving down mountain slopes that encircle the village. Don Paco put his arm around me and said they were people coming to the funeral. They came from the upward-flowing valley of *Los Trigales* — the wheat fields — out of mud-homes sprinkled upon its golden breast. They came from high forests where the sounds of axe and machete were quiet this day. They came from where genteel waterfalls known as Las Grutas splashed them in happy times, and they came from the hamlet of Chiul, which I had run through on a sweet night 12 years before and from where the boy's killer had come. They came in homage to the *gran patojo* — best boy — who would have been the first Mayan in this village to attend college.

In the absence of radios, TVs, phones, and even electricity, they had heard the news of his killing lip-to-ear from a neighbor or a wanderer like don Paco. The news traveled fast — it had to because a body must be buried quickly lest the dear one's last memory be of stink; but some heard it last-minute and hurried so they could make it in time to kneel upon the church floor and feel in their moment of pain a kinship with those who possessed the forever hurt. A few came not knowing why two unmelodious church bells kept banging.

Don Paco patted my back.

"*Ven,* Terry....Come, it's time to visit the dead boy."

He led me up the road past the town square to an adobe house where people gathered outside. On a broad earth expanse, about 50 children played. Some older ones sat at a table passing around a deck of cards.

We entered the open door to see an open casket illuminated by candles casting warmth on the boy's serene, young, young, young face. Huge floral sprays surrounded the casket, and Indian men and women on their knees surrounded the flowers, chanting the rosary in high-pitched sing-song voices as a man with a taut smile swung a can on a rope boiling with incense-scented clouds that filled the room. Sobs of despair burst from the parents — from their mouths, from their chests, from the very center of the earth.

And that is how it had gone all night until sunrise brought a final mournful "Aieee!" from the father. He and his bent-over wife paid their respects to all and made their way through chanting villagers outside across the plaza and up the road to the cemetery where they oversaw the construction of their son's final room. It would be different than all those hundreds of others: row after row of body-length and shoulder-width mounds whitewashed to gleam day and night in the eyes of travelers on the high-mountain road above Cunén. By contrast the boy's home was in the top right space of a commodious, blue-and-white brick structure that held five other residents.

The father, in a calm voice, suggested a few changes as workmen completed the final preparations, and then we returned to his house.

The mourning went on all day as people came in shifts, praying and eating until, at around 5 p.m., the dead boy's schoolmates at Escuela Devarones — a public school built after Ayuda's — gathered on the street in four orderly lines stretching 75 feet. They numbered about 300, all wearing school uniforms. Four girls at the head of the procession held bunches of white daisies and pink geraniums with polished green leaves.

Clouds heavy with the gray of rain rose over the mountain as if on cue.

It was so hard for children to wait in line without murmuring and fidgeting as they watched the doorway from where incense poured. Three scrawny dogs with their tails down loped out upon a pathway of rocks and dirt and crackly corn husks and started circling the students. A tiny boy in rubber galoshes came and stared up at me as I scribbled in my notebook that on its cover had a gaily painted portrait of a blond girl in a checkered pinafore holding a basket of spring flowers. Weathered old Mayan women stood kind of hunched along the stone curbs, and interspersed among them sat patrulleros (men forced to 'defend' their village against rebels) in dirtied, rough white cotton pants and shirts, clutching their old M1's. One of them greeted Hector.

"Hola, don Paco."

A slightly drunk man wobbled over and said he knew me. "Didn't you work in the clinic years ago with Dorotea?"

"Yes." I was astonished that someone remembered.

"Si, si, te recuerdo," he said. "Do you have 35 centavos for a bottle of cusha? Remember how we used to drink together?"

I dug out a dollar, enough for almost three bottles, he returned to his friends, and they all went to a tienda and missed the funeral, which began with the mother and father serving coffee in bright blue plastic cups to those inside. The casket emerged on the shoulders of the boy's closest friends, who circled the house for his last goodbye before lowering the coffin to the ground. A man in a wide brim hat with square-edge nails held in his whiskered lips hammered the cover shut with three sharp raps to each nail head. When his hammer went silent, the boys re-hoisted their friend and solemnly walked into the center of the processional lines as mom and dad and brother walked to the front, weeping, followed by an old bent woman with an enormous basket of flowers on her head. Murmuring became chanting and crying morphed into singing as the procession moved in slow, measured, rhythmic steps to the church a couple of blocks away. The family cook wailed into her handkerchief as the procession passed by.

The boys with the casket were first to walk up the low broad step of the church, past the very point where their burden was shot, led by two altar boys with tall white candles. *I was an altar boy like them once.* The priest with a brass can of incense on a silver chain greeted the coffin at the altar, swinging sweet-smelling arcs of smoke. *I once studied to be a priest.* After the family entered heads down, 300 mostly Indian women crowded in, kneeled on the hard tile floor, and sang out the entire rosary for about a half hour.

Suddenly, Hector hissed and pointed to a moth the size of a hummingbird fluttering about. "A death moth! It carries the souls of the dead. Aieee, does it carry the boy's?" I spied a distinct skull-like image on the moth's back and felt his fear.

The rosary ended and a man with a nasal voice led a song — answered at the height of the kneeling women's high-pitched voices — that would cut to the softest part of the hardest heart and squeezed mine as if trying to revive my Catholic faith. The procession re-shaped outside as those gray clouds sagged down the mountain just above the village, loosing big drops to splash here and there in the dust of a road upon which hundreds of mostly bare feet shuffled in two lines behind the coffin carriers toward the cemetery. The mourners entered its plain, wrought iron gates, sprinkled themselves among the graves and high hillocks, and joined in a final, pining song that died out as the school principal stepped forward to speak.

The cemetery

"What a boy," he declared. "A fine student. A great human being who took on so much responsibility. Un gran patojo!"

He bowed, stepped over to Hector, and whispered, "Hola, don Paco."

Hundreds of female voices cried out as classmates grunted in their struggle to insert the boy's casket. Finally, it slid in with a gravelly sound and they placed upon it the school's blue banner, stepping back as two workmen with trowels reverently closed the entrance, caressing mortar in between the bricks with their fingertips. As they worked, the father stepped atop a dirt mound, stretched up his arms and face to the weeping clouds, and cried out in Spanish:

"My blood!

"My body!

"My bones!

"My people!

"My SON!"

His body jerked with each stabbing cry, as if the bullet that killed his son was piercing him over and over, and I too twitched as it ricocheted into me. After a pause, the father lowered his head and voice to speak words that soon would echo in the voice of a woman atop a faraway volcano.

"We are all equals...those who are rich, those who are poor, those who are Indian, those who are ladino, those who are Norteamericanos. There is no difference among us. We are all the same. The man who shot the gun...The man who gave him the gun...The boy who was shot with the gun.

"MY SON!"

Two men came to steady the father as he ended with a

few words in the clicking tongue of his Mayan people. They told me later he expressed gratitude to the North American people, naming Morse and Dorotea, who had been so helpful to the people.

Hector and I were among the last to leave as the cemetery slowly emptied, until only a quiet figure remained atop a mound of dirt, head down in the rain. We walked past the coffin-maker who took off his baseball cap with its crudely drawn skull and crossbones and nodded respectfully.

"Hola, don Paco."

The Poet's Lesson

Hector dropped into his padded wooden chair that night, sighing like a punctured truck tire as his body melted into the chair's contours. We were in the covered courtyard of his little house, illuminated by a bit of light leaking from under the door — just enough to reflect perspiration on his brow and rain drops dripping from the eaves. As the sigh weakened, his chin drooped and Hector dozed.

What an unrealized man this self-proclaimed poet of Cunén was. Everything he tried came from his heart, if not from talent. His poetry, dazzling with sincerity, had neither rhythm nor rhyme. His artwork was awful. He couldn't draw and even when he traced the simplest subject, the effort was a scrawl. He had the softest hands of any man, woman and child in Cunén, and the softest heart. He had never swung a hoe or a machete. The only work he had ever done was here and there for 20 years as a clerk in his brother's store, who hustled at the counter as Hector mostly dreamed in the back room; a brother who had the village's only TV that now was blank because, while Hector could watch it, he had no skills to fix it; a brother who became one of the richest men in the village by profiting off every bit of candy and cigarettes and cusha he sold even as Hector found ways to give away such items for nothing.

And yet, everywhere we went all were reverent to him. To them he wasn't Hector but don Paco, who listened from his heart to all the things they had to say and all the things they had no words to say, and chatted with them heart to heart. I said both of his names outloud as he slept. One gargled in my throat: "Hector." The other fluttered off my tongue: "Don Paco."

He didn't rouse, but others did.

Tiny dots of light rose from bushes behind his slumbering self...blinking, little dots that floated upward until they created a perfect backdrop that his body seemed cut out of...framing him, haloing him as if he was a saint or an angel or simply the essence of good.

"Don Paco." I spoke softly, yet with such awe that he awoke and saw the tiny flickers and breathed out their name.

"*Loo-see-air-nah-gaaz*" — luciernegas — as beautiful a word to my ear as to the eyes of don Paco.

"AIEEE!"

Suddenly, his left hand clutched his chest as he stabbed his right hand toward a dark shape creeping up the door behind me.

"*Murcielago*!"

He saw a creature of death come to snatch a soul, perhaps his. I saw a bat and chewed its delightful name, *mooor-see-eh-la-go,* as Hector grabbed a broom and swatted frantically at the poor creature until it escaped through a crack atop the door. The bat in Mayan mythology is a symbol of demons and death.

Then he sat down, breathing hard, and looked up at me.

"You don't know how to see, Terrry."

His soft-spoken words sucker-punched me.

"What, Hector....what...what do you mean?"

"In that time before when you were here, I watched you secretly through the curtains of my brother's tienda. Watched you walk up and down the street, looking at everything and seeing nothing. Talking to everyone but not seeing them."

His voice trailed off as his eyes half-closed, as my eyes tried to pierce into his thoughts and understand what he meant.

"It is getting dark, don Paco. We need to go inside and rest for tomorrow."

He was already deep inside himself, so I crept off to bed, wondering what I was too blind to see and thinking about the day to come. Don Paco had agreed to guide me south along a road dotted with war refugees fleeing north, the same road many of today's poverty refugees flee north on. I had wanted us to head the other direction to Nebaj, but Don Paco refused. *Too many soldiers...Thousands of people dead in its mountains...The fiercest guerrillas live up there — the ones who attacked Cunén two years ago...The war is more tranquilo to the south.*

The chicken bus arrived early the next morning with its belches of diesel smoke and blaring of horn and took us to the small village of Chicaman after a harsh day of mountain travel on rutted dirt roads not much wider than the bus. Unknown to me was that a young Mayan woman named Rigoberta Menchu lived near here with her family, deep in the forest but not deep enough to avoid being targeted by marauding, raping, killing soldiers. Her book about those travails would help her win the Nobel Peace Prize, but all I knew is that Chicaman is from where the young Carlos came, and told don Paco of my failed attempt to make him a TB healer 12 years before.

"Aieee, it is worse than you think," don Paco instantly replied. "Carlos died of too much cusha. Your Ayuda trained another young man, Diego, as a dentist — the first full-time dentist in Cunén. Perhaps not the best, but the only one. The people called him a pliers dentist. All he could do was pull teeth without anesthesia."

"Sounds bad."

"It's worse than bad. He also liked cusha too much. He drank so much that his clinic only stayed open three days a week. Then two. Then none." Diego died of alcoholism last year, he said with a sigh. Now Cunén had no dentist, no doctor, no volunteers like Dorotea and Morse and — looking at me — no Terry. All the norteamericans fled the violence. Every now and again some missionaries, wearing white shirts and skinny ties, came through, but they were just here to harvest souls.

I sighed, too. Carlos and Diego were tragic symbols of how hard it is to achieve anything of lasting impact in the country. Morse had warned me of that when I grew impatient with the daily grind of do-gooderism. Patience, he said. Rome wasn't built in a day, he said. I thought of Nebaj's weaver women who spend their days taking one stitch after another. They don't curse each dropped stitch but dream of what someday will be born — a cloth of such beauty that people come from around the world to buy it.

We decided to spend the night at a pension, where the owner became agitated as he made our beds. Two nights ago, 20 or so soldiers led by a lieutenant broke down the door of his shop and put a machine gun to his head, threatening to kill him if he didn't provide a car or truck to take them back to their base. He didn't have one so they left with a promise they would soon return and kill him.

On the way we had been stopped several times by hapless patrulleros who walked around the bus like cops checking for broken lights and bald tires. Patrulleros are village men forced into service as unwilling militia protectors of their villages against communists. Some have old rifles like the one used to kill Juan Botón. The others will have machetes or just sticks, yet this motley corps is a fiendishly effective protector of the army against guerrillas.

"Pendejos!" The driver cursed into their ears and left them standing awkwardly.

Up the road we were stopped by soldiers who forced everyone out for an ID check. Their leader treated everyone with contempt, almost spitting in our faces, and when he saw I was a reporter looked ready to shoot, but only sneered and waved us on.

The driver carefully drove out of earshot before cursing, "Pendejos!"

"Fuck the army," the shop owner said when I told him.

"Fuck them all," said a middle-aged man standing nearby. By all he meant the soldiers and guerrillas. "They are all terrorists and the patrulleros are caught in the middle." The army used patrulleros as guards surrounding the army posts and camps, and often were the ones first killed when guerrillas attacked.

The next day, after six hours of horror driving in monsoon wind and rain, we came to the slightly larger village of San Cristobal, where a father and son disagreed about whether it was an honor to be a patrullerro. Three years before, the son was forced to guard a road to an army base when guerrillas shot out his left eye. He rubbed the empty socket bitterly as he spoke of how patrulleros were unpaid soldiers who got their asses kicked while the army hid behind them.

A sad woman in her 40's, the daughter of those whose house we stayed in, said her husband had been shot dead by the guerrillas, forcing her and her four kids. to live off her aged parents. At least 100 peasants had been killed — caught between the guerrillas and the army. Her story added to my growing consternation over violence by guerrillas. They were supposed to be the good guys in a land where the army slaughtered Mayans.

Back on the bus for the rough overnight return trip to Cunén, don Paco suddenly leaned over to speak in a hushed voice of why he so loved the native people. His hands fluttered as he spoke words that fluttered my heart.

"As a baby I sucked at the teat of a Mayan woman whose own child had died. Her milk was my blood and my blood is now Mayan."

Dear God, I hadn't expected this, pausing before I stammered how I understood.

He looked at me sharply.

"You understand nothing about my land and my people because you don't see why we suffer and live as we do. You come and go, but we stay. Until you stay and be with us and see who we really are you cannot know us."

It was not a rebuke but a truth and I took it that way, knowing that I was going to leave Cunén soon. The bus banged along up the road like my inner conflicts until the road topped out on the mountain and tipped down toward a dazzling sight.

"Aieee, Terry, look!"

A valley of light lay below.

"Such an incredible village it must be."

"No, Terry, look again."

We plunged into a sea of flickering, pulsating drops of light that swirled as we passed through, and our faces glowed.

"Luciernagas..."

Don Paco breathed out that magic word as if he was praying.

"Loo-see-ehr-nah-gaaz," I responded, each syllable twinkling within me like the creatures outside, lit up by their feelings, for this was a gathering of lovers we had interrupted so rudely. Alone, each would blink erratically but here in their millions they pulsed like a single, beating heart as the driver slowed to roll through a shallow river, its stones shimmering with wet light cast upon them by our passage, and like the river the luciernegas seemed to flow down the mountain up against us in full flood, catching in the rough edges of doors and hood and windows as we floated upwards, leaving thousands spinning as tornadoes of light in the vortex of our passage. The bus emerged brightly strung as if by Christmas lights, and I imagined how my superstitious friend might react if he was watching from a distance as our flashing apparition moved up the mountain side. "Aieee," he might say, "un barco fantasma!" A ghost ship. But he was gawking and as voiceless as I was, both of us awed by the purest beauty we had ever seen, unblemished by the cruelty that darkened his world. Our eyes at last embraced the same vision, unable to close until the last luciernega blinked out.

Worn by the day and its closing scene, we slumbered against each other and I started dreaming of the young, dark-haired beauty back in Chicaman who was the boldest of three young ones grouped around me, asking my name, whether I had a girlfriend, and making it obvious in so many flirty ways that they were available. I was flattered but knew I was nothing more than a tall, white escape from their circumstances. "Here, Terrry," the beauty said, trilling my name as she offered me three ripe purple plums. Her soft red lips smiled as I bit into one and felt its juice drool down my chin.

I awoke and thought of the dark-haired woman I had left behind to come here — the bluegrass singer who kept sending me letters, urging me to come home soon because...she couldn't wait forever. She disappeared as deep sleep took over, and I awoke in the early light as the bus entered Cunén, horn blaring.

Don Paco grabbed my hand as I stepped from the bus.

"This is your last day here, Terry, you must say goodbye to Cunén."

And so we set off again, as we had most days in my time here with Don Paco. By now I realized that he was the voice of Cunén, its very heart and soul and chronicler, and beloved by all. Each day he took me to aldeas I never knew existed, where people asked how it is in the world of Cunén and he told them the latest gossip, the latest local political nonsense, the latest newness that has come over the mountain into the village — like me. In some places he introduced me but in others I was humbled at not needing introduction.

"Oh, Terrry, we remember you and Ayuda. When are you all coming back? We need you." A woman's voice was calling for me to enter and have coffee. "Do you remember when you used to sit with us before and share stories?" Who could forget. A fire burned in the center of her mud-floored home and smoke went straight up through the fronds of the roof. Coffee beans had boiled in the pot all night, and hunks of cane sugar were tossed in, along with pots of cream or milk. It tasted like Cunén.

As I traveled with this self-taught and heartfelt poet, awkward artist, foot-leather philosopher, and son of his village, I pondered what he could do if the world was right. And that's when it hit me. Newspaper editor!

Just before returning here, I had spent years in a small farm town as a newspaper reporter and editor. One gets very close to the people in such a place. Cunén is a very small farm town and who could be closer to it than Don Paco? If only Cunén had a printing press! He would be the ideal newspaper writer/editor/editorialist/gossip columnist. It's what he already did on foot and by voice. Imagine if he had the power of a press. He could name his newspaper "The Cradle" - which is what he says the word Cunén means. Imagine, he could write an entire edition based just on our final day together:

The poet

The Cradle!

Cunén - Too Poor To Have Beggars

There is only one beggar in our village. Her name is Maria. You have seen her sitting in her torn skirt and unwashed sad huipile. She has one front tooth, but why does she need more? She has so little food to chew. And why does our little village have only one beggar when the grand Guatemala City has them everywhere? Because most of us are poor and barely have enough. We all would be beggars in the grand city. Here our little something is enough. Maria has even less - a tooth.

Gringo Terry Helps Build Bridge As Mayor Watches

Have you seen gringo Terry from the United States walking around? He is tall and must not eat so much because he is so skinny. Many people remember when he lived here and was with Ayuda and helped us - before the war chased them away.

I was taking him down our once-magnificent main road into town that is nothing but ruts and holes now - thanks to our excellent Mayor. Should we call him Señor Ruts and Rocks? I was showing gringo Terry the road and suddenly a group of our fine volunteer road builders - 50 of them - started yelling: "Hola, Terry. Hola, gringo. Did you come to help us build this bridge?" Yes, our gringo friend said, although his back hurt from playing with patojos all morning. The men were trying to drag a giant 40-foot-long log into place and needed more muscles. He joined in. Aieee, how they all chanted and struggled to move that monster. Aieee, how slowly it came. But inch by inch they got it almost in place when our grand Mayor appeared with his nice clean pants and his nice combed and oiled hair and his fine white shirt. He stopped and gave such good advice: "Just a little bit more that way, hombres." Then he said, "Con permiso," and walked on the log to go to his special place - perhaps his mistress. Our poor workers spent hours finally getting the log just right. Poor Terry went to my house and laid down with an aching back.

Our Basketball Team Has No Basketballs

Such a wonderful basketball team we have - we almost beat the champion team from Quiche. We would have if our team had practiced. The team would have practiced if they had a basketball. How can you practice without a basketball? Like actors. Our poor team runs up and down the court pretending to dribble and shoot. Aieee, imagine how good we could be with a basketball!

Cusha Kills - Beware!

Poor Domingo Cantu who lives high up in Los Trigales where the wheat grew thick as a patojo's hair until the Mormons left and we had no more fertilizer. Now there are such poor, thin, little stalks of wheat - like Domingo himself. Gringo Terry and I visited Domingo this week in his little adobe house, which was dark and cold because he no longer can go up the mountain to cut firewood. He saw Terry and started crying for once he and Terry used to drink cusha together and would dance and be happy. But now Domingo is broken and cannot work because of too much hard work and cusha. Terry quit drinking cusha when he left and now look how tall he is. So many cusha drinkers are broken or breaking. Look at Terry, I tell them. Maybe if you quit drinking cusha you could be tall like him.

Don Paco's Poet Corner

"Oh, Cunén, hidden paradise, in your nights the stars appear as pearls, illuminating my tranquil and shining soul...You are a rest for every aching heart, a nest of love for all."

Why The War Leaves Us Alone

Gringo Terry and I just returned from visiting the villages south of Cunén - aieee, they suffer so much from the guerrillas and the army. In San Cristobal, hundreds of poor campesinos were killed. We didn't dare go north where so many thousands have been killed.

Remember two years ago when the guerrillas came from the north and blew up our building and killed 10 of us and chased our mayor — the good one — up the mountain? We didn't raise our fists because we learned long ago when the Spanish came down our road on their horses to not be foolish. We knew the army soon would come down that road and chase away the guerrillas. And they did. Remember?

We don't need the guerrillas. We don't need the army. We need the norteamericanos to come back with seed and fertilizer and medicine. Maybe gringo Terry can tell them to come back. Maybe he will come back.

Special Report: Sheka Is Worth Dying For

Recently, on the road to Quiche, guerrillas stopped our chicken bus and ordered everyone out. Aieee, Dios! They shot the driver and a soldier and placed fire bombs under the bus. Then they came to me with their guns and I thought I would never see my beloved little village again.

"Who are you?" they said. "You look too soft to be a hard-working campesino."

"Aieee, I am just a poor man with nothing but my sheka bread."

"Sheka?" They seemed so surprised. Si, I told them it was on the bus. They licked their lips. The whole world knows about Cunén's special sheka — so special that one must never feed it to dogs because once having tasted it they will die of hunger before eating tortillas again. "Hurry," the guerrilla said. "Save the sheka."

"I did. And we all ate our dear bread in the warmth of the burning bus."

———————

The sheka bread story made me laugh, though he told it on the verge of tears.

"You were lucky," I told him.

"Aieee. Lucky once. But my life is full of bad luck. My brothers and father had all the good luck. My brother owned a store and had the only TV in town. And had 100 shirts and many shoes. Look at what I wear." He wears the same soiled clothes he's worn since I came here.

"My older brother kept careful records of all the women he slept with — 87! All ladinas. Aieee, I only had 66. All Mayans."

Any other guy telling that story would tell it for laughs, but Hector was serious.

"He was so much luckier than me."

The old woman cleaning our table rolled her eyes and mocked his way of talking.

"Aieee, poor don Paco, how unlucky you are. Your whole family gets to sleep at the cemetery and you are forced to sleep here."

"Si, but..."

As he started detailing his many physical ailments, I got up. I had heard them before.

"I am tired, don Paco, and must rise early. I am leaving in the morning."

"Aieee! Everyone leaves me."

That last night, alone in my bed, by the light of a candle, I wrote:

"To quote Fitzgerald and paraphrase Hemingway: 'The poor are different from the rest of us...They have less money.' There is nobility in striving, in working, in fighting the odds, but nobility dims when one's struggle, at best, keeps you in just one place all your life....They work, work, work all day, motivated by the most important commandment: Thou shalt eat."

I put down the pen, wondering if I was finally beginning to see.

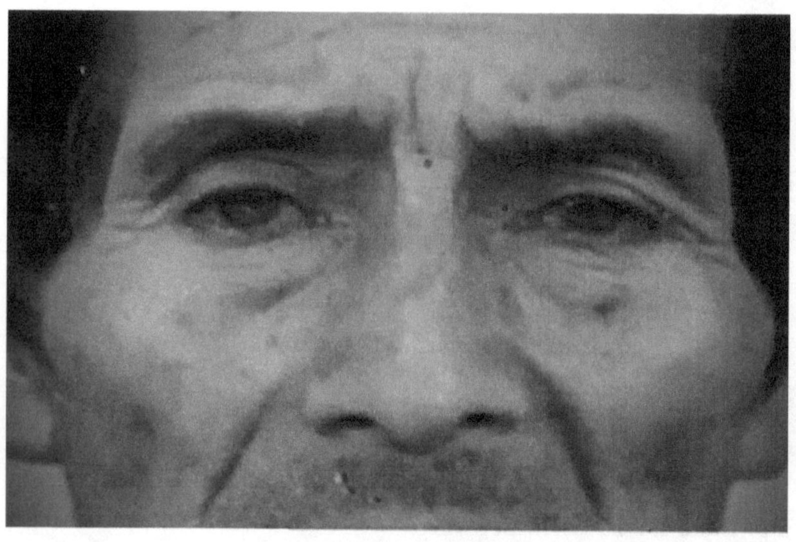

The eyes of Juan Boton

It was tomorrow and the dead boy's father spoke of how the bullet did more than kill his son. We were alone in don Paco's house as I packed to leave Cunén. He was composed and earnest.

"Senor Terry, do you know about the Mayan social security system?"

"No."

"It is like this....A father works hard all his life, digging in his steep field so that he can save money to send one son to school. The boy goes away. One day, many years later, the father is working in the field and feels his son's hand upon his shoulder. 'Get up, father. Drop your hoe. Come home. Sit in your chair. You have worked hard all your life for me. Now, I will work hard for you.' "

Juan Botón's eyes were a gateway to the entire Mayan world and for just a brief, brief, brief instant they invited me in. In that mote of time that lasted no longer than the flash of a firefly, I was on the mountain hoeing, on the grave wailing, in the church praying to an agonized, twisted ceramic body as nailed to his cross as the people were to their circumstances. *A miracle, Jesus, please...a miracle.*

Not a miracle, but a bus was coming. I heard it rumbling and already the driver was pulling on the horn. I rose to meet it, but the father held me with his gaze.

"Promise me you will never forget my family...and our village."

"*Nunca!*" I vowed. Never.

The father left, trotting. He had work to do. There was one more son.

The first time I left Cunén, I walked sprightly up the road this bus crawled up, whistling from my heart. What a time it had been among the Maya. We had such good times. Worked hard together. Had some happy cusha moments. Built a school. Grew some crops. Told stories. Created stories. Laughed. Cried. How good I felt then for my good deeds. Good enough to walk 50 miles and write a song about it.

There was no whistling this time as the bus took me past don Paco, who had turned his back because he was too sad to watch me leave. The bus zigged up the mountain and I pulled out a paper on which he had written a poem to me — not good but precious, and though it has long since disappeared, I feel it in my bones.

Cunén was gone when I looked up.

I started coughing about halfway back, hacking up the same white stuff the old man on the chicken bus had coughed on me. Fortunately, I was staying in a doctor's house, but it took six weeks to recover, and at some point as I lay gasping in bed, the young Mayan housekeeper lit candles around me, praying on her knees that God would wrap me in his arms. Grateful am I that God was busy elsewhere.

And, there was a letter from the bluegrass singer. I had left her, saying, *I don't know how long I will be gone or even whether I am coming back.* That was five months ago. She had written many supportive, loving letters in that time. I had written a few but not for awhile. Her latest letter had a different tone. There were some fellows hovering around that she had discouraged, except for one. He, too, was a bluegrass singer. A nice guy. She liked him. *Please hurry home, Terry.*

When I finally was able to stand and walk, weeks later, nothing mattered more than heading to my cafe hangout, Doña Luisa's, where I started typing the story of how one village and one father anguished when one boy was slain in a land of slaughter.

Where Are The Guerrillas?

September 1985

ORPA guerrillas

The Englishman

I was typing on the world's first portable computer, a tablet called the "Model 100" by its maker and "Trash 80" by journalists who loved and loathed it. It had a tiny little screen big enough for one long sentence or two short ones if you wrote simple like a journalist should, and it made a unique tapping noise when you typed, but I never heard it in stereo before, and looked up.

Across the stone-paved courtyard, a skinny white dude in his late twenties with spectacles was hunched over his Trash 80, pecking away. He looked up, spied my Trash 80, and instantly lit up.

"Hey," he said.

"Hey."

"I'm Ambrose."

"Terry."

"I'm a journalist."

"Me, too."

He grabbed his Trash 80 and came over, quick-moving and fast-talking in a cultivated English accent, and placed it on the glass-topped table even as he grabbed a chair from behind and dragged it clattering over the stones under his butt.

"Why are you coughing?" asked my instant, best, new friend.

"Pneumonia. Been down 6 weeks."

"I just got over hepatitis and had to go back to England to heal. Took six months. Who you writing for?"

"Couple of small California papers. You?"

"San Francisco Examiner. The Economist in England. Wire services. Why'd you come?"

"I took a two-week trek alone in the High Sierras and dreamed of Mayan friends caught up in the war. Had to see what happened to them. You?"

"I walked alone across Africa and decided to come to Central America for the revolutions. El Salvador, Nicaragua. Covered them. Came here looking for guerrillas. The government swears they crushed them."

We were caught in a one-upmanship contest and he was crushing me.

"Uh, I just came back from the Nebaj area looking for guerrillas. People told me they are still active."

"Nebaj? I was planning to go up there and look for a friend — another journalist — who disappeared looking for them there. I was supposed to go with him but got the hepatitis."

The unspoken question hung in the air between us.

Within days we were on the road in a rented Subaru wagon with a passionate socialist radio journalist from Spain in a dash through Guatemala toward a rendezvous with rebels.

Return To Shangri-La

Screams erupted behind me from the back seat where Ambrose was rolled up in terror.

"You're going to kill us, you fucking Spanish twat!"

Ambrose shouted what my constricted throat could not as Francisco — the fierce-talking, fierce-driving Spaniard — hunched over the wheel with his accelerator foot to the floor, refusing to retreat in the face of a head-on collision with a car hurtling downhill toward us. We were passing, uphill, a tractor-trailer truck grinding along just a tick slower than our grossly underpowered little Subaru. Francisco was driving after cursing the too-slow way that Ambrose had been driving. Now he was cursing at our car for being too slow. A dropoff was on our left, the semi on our right, but the Spaniard was at a bullfight — Christ, he was the bull! — refusing to back down as the adversary bore down upon us. I closed my eyes and lowered my head.

Brakes squealing, car swerving, Ambrose cursing, me wanting mommy...

Francisco jerked over at the last second and pulled to the side of the road as Ambrose repeatedly and loudly demanded to drive, and within minutes felt the wrath of two passengers who thought they would die of boredom at the pace he drove.

And so it went as a car full of roosters pecked at each other along the road I had ambled up weeks before by chicken bus in a much more mellow and heartfelt mood. When we reached a flat stretch of gravelly country road, I insisted on driving, based upon years of driving such roads in a farm town, and immediately skidded us into a ditch against barbed wire. We all got out to push the car back up to the highway where Ambrose jumped in the driver seat and drove us toward a wide, deep pond of water on the road, exclaiming that if you drove fast enough the car would float across. Francisco and I both yelled as the car struck the water, sending a wave over the hood, and became a boat. Through the windshield wipers we saw the other side drift close and felt our wheels touch ground. Ambrose exulted, punching the accelerator to speed us around a swooping curve that looked familiar, then swerve us left to avoid the mountainside, and there it was below us — the magical Nebaj.

But where was the magic I had felt 12 years ago when I first looked upon it with untutored eyes?

Maybe it was the maniacal driving or the presence of my rough companions or that something had changed in how I viewed the world or because I already knew of the horrors inflicted on Nebaj. It just lay there as we streaked toward it, flying past that point where grim men with torches had run off the mountain and daggered me with hard looks in 1973. I since learned they might have been members of a guerrilla group festering among those high, hidden places; a group the Melvilles tried to hook up with when it was first coming together in Mexico, whose seven-member vanguard secretively entered Guatemala the same year I first arrived, and gathered Mayans into full-on rebellion until the army swept them back into hiding and punished the natives with massacre. The same army awaiting us as we entered the village.

A machine gun emplacement forced us to stop at the edge of town central where once I had seen baskets of the greenest beans and the reddest radishes. A few Mayan women carrying tortillas and fabrics on their heads hardly glanced at us as they trotted by on the broken concrete road. A guard looked over our IDs and shook his head. No, we can't go into the town center. We drove a couple of blocks to another gun emplacement.

No.

Then another.

No.

I sensed Francisco's irritation. At the next emplacement, he blew up, screaming in Spanish so fast and loud and red-faced at the guard that both Ambrose and I traded fearful looks. People were shot for less in this land of tyranny. The guard's wide eyes spoke a different story, though —*He* was afraid — and let us in.

"What did you tell him?"

"To get fucked. I used an expression, *hace polvo*, we say in Spain — to 'make dust like a rabbit.' Those are fighting words to a Spaniard. I think he understood."

Soldiers wearing red berets, crisp camouflage uniforms, machine guns, and smirks swaggered about as we parked the car. They were the first Kaibiles I had seen, but I had heard about them. Kaibiles were trained by our Green Berets to be their Red Berets. Trained to have no pity, trained in torture and "psy-op" terror tactics, and anti-commie killing. Trained to do in Guatemala what our soldiers did in Vietnam — to "pacify" villages. They were our front line against communism in Guatemala just as the South Vietnamese were in Southeast Asia and the Contras were in Nicaragua. Contras and Kaibiles were the freedom fighters Ronald Reagan spoke of on TV with avuncular ignorance. Kaibiles were implicated in some of the worst massacres, killing entire villages of Mayans and tossing their corpses into water wells or onto burning piles. A red hat politely pointed out his comandante, the hefty major with thick mustache who was showing two middle-age white women around with gracious flourishes. We begged pardon and asked about Ambrose's lost companion.

"Si," the major said, studying our faces. "I have heard of Nicholas Blake and the other gringo he was with. They were last seen on top of a chicken bus headed up in the mountains. We did an exhaustive search and have concluded...he was killed by guerrillas."

But, Ambrose protested, the Army claims it killed all the guerrillas.

"There are a few that escaped deep into the mountains where your friend went. They don't like surprise visitors."

Then the major invited us to go visit the "model villages" built to house survivors of a scorched-earth policy his men had conducted throughout these mountains a few years before. The army wiped out dozens of Mayan villages, sometimes massacring everyone in a strategy that echoed what Mao did in China and what the U.S. did in Vietnam. Mao called it draining the sea in which the fish swam. The U.S. called it pacification. Millions of Chinese and Vietnamese and tens of thousands of Mayans were slaughtered.

The major went back to flirting as we went back to our Subaru.

Ambrose was in a dark mood.

"The Army killed him. I feel certain."

It was getting late, so we rented a room at Tres Hermanas — 'Three Sisters' — pension and I went walking about Nebaj. Except for the structures, it was not as I remembered when viewing it with brighter, younger eyes. There was no market on this day, no weavings, no entreating Mayan women, and few tourists. There was a brothel where a sergeant drunkenly taunted me to try the wares, and he would pay. Women in the house were slapping their soiled underwear in a pila — a concrete communal water basin — and looking at me with taut smiles. They would have been laughing little girls 12 years before, running around barefoot in the handwoven colors of their village. Now they wore rough white underclothes as they slapped laundry like they were making tortillas, and my gut clenched. The whole Mayan world was getting raped — was I going to join in? And then there was the matter of the girl I left behind, the bluegrass singer who was keeping the home fire warm.

"No gracias."

The sergeant growled something about no *huevos* (balls) as I went outside to breath afternoon air scented by cooking fires throughout the village, and took a cleansing stroll on a narrow graveled road through rows of mostly adobe, white homes and small stores with little courtyards tucked behind where fires were tended by mothers and daughters. I wasn't really looking for anything and that's how I found it.

The red belt.

It was as if the woman holding it had been waiting for my return all these years. She even looked like that tall, regal woman from the magic time with braids of hair and colorful ribbon encircling her head like a crown. The intense reds of her woven blouse, sprinkled with splashes of yellows and blues, were echoed in the belt draped over her right forearm. Its tied tassled ends nearly brushed her brown toes, sticking out from under the hem of her long, red, blue-striped skirt. She stood on a corner across the street and motioned me over with the fingers of her left upturned hand.

"It is a wedding belt," she said, but of course I already knew.

I took the precious object in my fingers and caressed it, tracing the faces of wolves and quetzal birds, amazed at the intricate artistry that flowed along much of its length. So much time and love had gone into its creation. I sighed. My funds were low. Almost every dollar in my pocket had been donated by the people of the small California farm town I had come from. They knew I didn't have enough money of my own to make this trip and set up a giving tree to make it possible. I had cried while plucking ones and fives and tens from its branches, but there wasn't enough for art even if it did cost only $20, which was the price a dozen years before. I returned the belt with deep feeling and gratitude.

"Gracias, señora, tan belleza" - so beautiful.

She grabbed my arm as I turned away.

"Barrato, señor!" - cheap.

Her face was hard and her voice urgent. Even desperate. She needed money. I didn't want to take advantage of her, but as I tried to turn way again she grabbed my left arm and laid the belt over it.

"What will you pay?"

"Please, señora."

"Please, señor!"

I walked away with the belt for about $4. Decades later, it hangs on my wall and I still feel like a thief.

The Search Continues

Ambrose wasn't ready to abandon his search for Nick no matter what the major claimed, so we stabbed deeper into the mountains above Nebaj in an area known as the Ixil Triangle, also called the red triangle for all the blood shed there in the civil war.

There was savagery on both sides and the people were caught between them, but whatever the guerrillas did was nothing compared to the army whose soldiers, many of them Mayan, were taught two things: how to kill and how to hate so that you wanted to kill. To hate the fucking godless communist motherfuckers who have invaded your land and swim among the people. They are coming for our minds and our wealth to turn us all into socialist slaves. They will steal our very patriotism. They are cancer that grows in healthy flesh — the flesh of the people. Cancer that, sadly, can only be removed by the knife, along with good flesh. Lastima. The people must die so that the country can survive this sickness sweeping the world. After awhile it makes sense, makes you not just capable but willing to kill for God and country.

Four hundred villages were swept from the earth and the survivors who didn't flee into mountain forests or across the

Mexican border were forced into those concentration camps, which so reminded me of camps the U.S. forced Japanese-Americans into during World War II.

Most people in the small villages and aldeas played dumb on the street when we asked about whether they had recently seen guerrillas or Nicholas. But, in the shadows and sanctuary of their homes, they whispered stories of being crushed between a massacring army and an increasingly feeble guerrilla resistance that no longer could protect them. They told of death and disappearances of fathers and sons and daughters and mothers, of rape and torture and murder. In the open sunlight they brightly smiled and offered blessings of *que la vaya bien* as we staggered about trying to comprehend each story. Yes, they whispered, there were guerrillas up there among the thickly forested highest slopes. Sometimes they snuck down, but not often, not in force, not like before when everyone thought victory was at hand. As for Nick...they shook their heads.

We drove upwards until the roads became too rutted, too narrow, too much like hiking trails into steep, thickly forested, mysterious heights. Finally, even Ambrose conceded his friend's likely fate — killed by someone — and we turned northwest toward Huehuetenango and other far-flung places where guerrillas had once held sway. *Way-way-ten-ongo*. What a happy-sounding taste it made within my memory, of walking 50 miles from my village in 1973 to this vast place of mountains and plains and valleys, writing a song as I went. Its chorus:

> *And the road is fer-de-lance in your legs*
> *And the sun dios del fuego,*

And you curse this day, this goddamned day,
On the way to Hue-hue-tenango

As I hummed, we zoomed along stretches of flat road, stopping at some of the larger villages to inquire about guerrilla activity — but we didn't randomly ask villagers on the street anymore. We talked to priests. My background as a Catholic seminarian loosened the mouth of almost every parish priest whose door we knocked on. Usually, they would have been more tight-lipped when talking to journalists, and for good reason — priests had been tortured, murdered and disappeared because the Army considered them sympathizers and supporters of the guerrillas.

"The Mayans are caught betwixt the divil and the deep blue sea, so to speak. And so are us priests and nuns. The guerrillas show up one day to preach the gospel of revolution. Then the army shows up and demands to know if we have been aiding the 'subversivos' as they call them. My job is to treat both sides like they are in my confessional. I listen and listen, then I say that the only outsider who regularly visits is the Holy Spirit himself on Sunday, and I invite them to Mass to meet him."

He acted as cartilage between the opposing forces and protected his flock by knowing all sides but taking none, unlike the Maryknoll Melvilles who rejected that role and took sides to end not just this moment of conflict but the continuing impact of hundreds of years of Mayan poverty.

The priest's leprechaun cunning usually worked, he said, but there was a time when his words could not slake the army's thirst for blood. Troops encircled a nearby village and forced dozens of people into the adobe church, which they locked and set afire. When the screams ended, soldiers pushed in the walls upon their bodies and left, having accomplished a good day's work against godless communists. One boy survived to crawl out of the smoldering rubble and tell the tale. Father Kelly found a safe place for him.

After more stories, the priest leaned across the table and advised us to quit searching for guerrillas in his area, where the army had so savagely crushed resistance. "If I were you, I'd head west toward Lake Atitlan. I hear that guerrillas control the volcanoes and mountains that surround the lake."

Good advice, the three of us decided, but sorrow and savagery slowed our journey.

The Song of Guatemala

As a journalist, before coming to Guatemala, I had seen many dead bodies that will forever haunt my memories, murdered by gun or knife, beheaded in an accident, drowned in rivers, burned in fires. Every body still lives in me, especially those of the young. I spent days in shock after pulling the broken body of a college student from a car wreck — the son of a beloved co-worker. But even more harrowing were the signs of dying and the sorrows of love lost to dying wrong. Dying right is our hope for our children...at the end of long, long lives. Juan Botón will always stand in the graveyard of my mind, crying out for his murdered son as rain and darkness fell.

High above the lake at Patzun, soldiers stopped us. "Momento," they said. They were clearing an accident.

It was no accident.

A tow truck dragged a pickup truck across the road in front of us and dumped it in a lot. It had a shot-out back window and what looked like blood on the side. We got out to investigate.

"Guerrilleros stopped it down the road and shot out its back window," a soldier said. "Two wounded tourists, a man and a woman, were forced out of the cab and killed."

The real story was told by fresh, bloody handprints on both front fenders, of wounded people using the truck for support, struggling hand over hand to the front where their prints smeared downwards in a final clawing grasp for life.

"Si, they were dressed like guerrilleros," said a witness. "But it was the first time I saw guerrilleros wearing shiny black army boots."

Late that afternoon, miles away in another village, we stopped at an army headquarters to ask about guerrilla activity. A young, easy-talking lieutenant said his men had recently swept the hills free of subversivos — up there, he pointed.

"Now all is tranquilo."

We went up there to check it out, up where adobe and wood-plastered homes were sprinkled about the hills, hidden by towering stalks of corn. Into the corn we plunged, feeling the slap of heavy ears and raspy leaves as we hiked blindly. Slap, slap, slap...

"There!" said the Spaniard. "Do you hear?"

From far away and high above came the faint sound of a woman singing. The singing lured us upward and was our compass through the corn, guiding us among the rows, pulling us nearer until the song became more of a tune without words, a silvery outpouring of notes from the heights of a soprano solo. Closer yet, the thatched roof of a campesino's home showed above the tassels, and we started hearing the truth. This was no song but the keening cry of a soul's despair, and it slowed us, made us reverent as we eased out of the corn into the home's courtyard where a young Mayan woman, black hair let down and glistening, sat with her face tilted upwards and her lips parted. A somewhat older Mayan woman came forward to greet us as yet another cry flowed forth.

"We have lost our husbands and fathers and sons and brothers," she said — all snatched in the middle of the night by the lieutenant's soldiers seeking guerrillas and collaborators. Dozens of men and boys had been taken from homes across these hills. A few had returned, but most were still gone and...anguish again sang out from its birthplace of pain.

The second woman shook her head and, staring at us with empty eyes from an expressionless face, said she had cried out every tear she had. Now, she wanted justice. She said it with such deadness, such lack of emotion, such stiffness of voice and spine, such deadly intent. Such cold fury. I had never encountered such a person so transformed, but she would not be the last.

As we made our way back down the hill, the young woman's cry became a song again. I think of it as the "Song of Guatemala" — beautiful, like the country, until you get too close. It was time to go to the volcanoes, my compadres and I agreed. Time to get closer.

We left imprinted with heartache, and I don't remember who was the driver as we drove Lake Atitlan's high perimeter, sucking in its magnificence for the first time, and understanding why Aldous Huxley called it "the most beautiful lake in the world" — blue as a Jay's breast, calm as a pond, almos encircled by the volcanoes I had seen from afar years before while running on the road from Nebaj, broiling with clouds and lightning and mystery.

Sprinkled around the base of three volcanoes were little villages that we all agreed should be our destination. We would start with the closest, whose tiny buildings dotted a fat thumb tip of land jutting into the lake. Close as it seemed from above, though, getting to San Lucas Toliman was a wrenching exercise of patience on rough roads that took a long, anxious hour to navigate before the road flattened at lake's edge and wound into town. We parked before the doors of the Catholic Church parish and knocked.

The large, gentle-faced fellow who answered the door was dressed more like a golfer than a priest, with those slightly rumpled slacks and short-sleeve shirt open at the neck, and he didn't act like the wisecracking mischievous Father Kelly as he absorbed my thin hand with his warm, large ones and pulled us into the waiting room next to his office

Father Greg brightened as I spoke of my time as a Maryknoll seminarian. He admired the Maryknolls for their work in the highlands among the Mayans and reacted warmly when I explained the mission we three were on.

"You have come to the right place. There is considerable guerrilla activity among these volcanoes, and a strong army presence along the lake's edge. You should talk to one of my priests who knows much about these affairs."

Father Kavanaugh, thinner but equally engaging, spoke to us in the back room, where we could be unobserved. For more than an hour we traded stories about things we had seen and experienced in this unsettled land. The church treads the situation delicately, he said. There are many heartaches to soothe among a people savaged by army brutality.

Father Greg

"The guerrillas of these volcanoes, a group called the Organization of the People in Arms or ORPA, are unlike other guerrillas in the country. They are sensible. They depend on popular support but they strive to keep the people from being caught between them and the army."

The chat was warm and informative and ended when the priest stood up and thanked us for coming, but as we were leaving, Father Greg pulled me aside and casually asked, "Do you want to meet them?"

The guerrillas!

Stunned, I could barely nod yes. My companions were shocked as well when I told them and we huddled at a local cafe, talking like schoolboys. Back at the rectory, we met with a collaborator who was clearly a campesino, dressed in rough woven white pantaloons striped lengthwise with blue lines. In a flat hard voice he asked about our backgrounds and looked at our press ids and left. Some minutes later Father Kavanaugh returned and sat in a chair across the table, looking serious.

"Come back tomorrow before sunset - and be prepared for a difficult climb and a long stay on the volcano."

We couldn't believe our good fortune and jabbered like patojos all the way back to Antigua. If things worked out, we would be the first journalists in three years to be with guerrillas in Guatemala. Our story could confirm that the army was lying about crushing the revolution. We dumped the rental car into the disbrelieving hands of the rental manager, who cried at seeing his mud-splattered, scratched and dented Subaru, and gasped at the odometer. "1,000 kilometers! You have driven everywhere!"

I didn't have the heart to tell him.

Up The Volcano

An airmail letter was in the fingers of the young Mayan housekeeper who had prayed over me for weeks when I was sick. She waved it in front of me, scenting the air with a familiar perfume.

"Su novia — your girlfriend?"

"Si!"

I snatched it from her, ripped it open, cringed at its message, stuffed it in a coat pocket, and raced to fill my backpack with necessities — a rainproof sleeping bag, some clothes, fresh reporters' notebooks, extra pens and my precious Italian hiking boots. *You took me to the top of the Sierra, now take me to the top of Guatemala*!

Light rain fell as I stumbled over the cobbled streets to Doña Luisa's, where a taxi waited with my anxious comrades.

"Vamonos!" said the Spaniard.

"I have to make a phone call."

In a phone booth I pulled Suzanne's letter from my coat pocket.

Things are moving fast...Please call, Terry!

Her message was clear: she had stayed true all these months while I was swallowed up in this country and rarely communicated back to her. She needed hope. Some drops splashed onto the ink and left a smear as I pondered what to do. Ambrose had an idea.

"Hurry."

I picked up the phone and stuck my finger in the rotary dial on the first digit of a number I knew by heart. Doors were opening to a new world. A phone call would keep the familiar one open. The dial twitched.

"Hurry!"

I hung up.

Three hours later, back in San Lucas Toliman, Father Kavanaugh opened the rectory door and ushered us quickly to a back room. He talked softly like the conspirator he was. "When I give you the signal, run and get into the back of a truck."

We huddled close on chairs, staring at each other. *Is this really happening? Did I just wake up in the pages of a Hemingway novel?* The pulse in my temple throbbed with the passage of time...time...time...

"It's here! Hurry, boys."

We grabbed our packs and raced through the door he held open.

"Go with God!"

In the twilight, a pickup truck with a camper shell awaited. We threw in our stuff and jumped in. As the truck rattled off, at a speed that wouldn't attract attention, its driver said we should immediately run into a cornfield when he stopped. We all breathed hard and looked into each other's wide eyes and said nothing as, perhaps, 10 minutes passed of swift rumbling.

The truck stopped.

The tailgate dropped.

It was nearly dark. Tall corn grew in rows to the road's edge. We jumped out. A campesino jumped from the passenger door and started running into the corn.

"Follow him," the driver hissed.

We ran through the rows for a couple of hundred yards to a tree.

"Wait here," the campesino said, leaving us as mist and darkness started to dissolve our surroundings. I heard my companion's fast breathing and felt my own. This isn't a Hemingway novel, it's my own true story. I am composed of words on the opening page of a great war chapter being written with my own footsteps, my own heartbeat, my own eyes. Visual, visceral, the smell of plowed earth and wet leaves, the birds unseen but twittering all about us, the mist that made long rows of corn melt in the distance along the base of this volcano named Toliman, a conjoined twin of the one named Atitlan behind it.

Suddenly, the birds screeched in a single voice as a dark figure emerged from the mist 100 feet away, flitting back and forth across the rows as it came toward us, getting larger. I choked down a cough. My lungs were still healing from pneumonia and that cigarette I just smoked didn't help.

"Amigos."

The campesino spoke in the hushed undertone we all would speak on the journey ahead, alerting us to stay quiet and follow him. After embracing each of us, he took off at an easy pace that I came to think of as the guerrilla trot. It never slowed, it never sped. Think of wolves loping along in single file, chasing the much-swifter elk. Mile after mile, up and down hills, through thick brush and flat plain, wearing down their prey until, exhausted, the elk turns to face death rather than take one more agonizing step. Gasping, choking, spitting, I kept the pace as we started moving uphill. It was a good path, easy to see in the starlight, and eventually, as the minutes and hours passed, my lungs calmed and the cough changed from hacking to a kind of soft huff.

Good, there is less chance of alerting army patrols.

Two hours and many strides blended as we moved through corn and coffee and thick, clinging bush. In rhythm we entered more densely forested terrain, took a sharp left, and plunged through bush into a small opening where five green-clad figures awaited, full of smiles, embraces and good cheer. Our trek was over!

"No, it has just begun," said their leader, a gaunt figure named Profane, his chosen war name to disguise his real identity. They were a patrol sent to take us the rest of the way, far up and around both volcanoes. We barely had enough time for cold gruel, some chat, and a smoke before taking off on the longest and, they warned, most treacherous part of the journey. There could be army ambushes or lurking spies called orejas — ears. We must run swift and silent, but I had foolishly smoked a cigarette and could not calm its cough.

"Shhh," said Otto, a stout young Mayan fellow who had transformed from pacifist to guerrilla when the army killed his brother.

I swallowed the next cough as our run resumed.

At first it was relatively pleasant on a well-laid path that took us up along a ridge on the volcano's open flank, with the lake spread out below and the twinkling lights of the village San Juan Toliman in full view. But we, too, were in full view on this ridge path and I turned to Otto running behind me.

"Otto, no wild animal would run like we are on this ridge - clearly visible to its hunters."

"Ha! Our hunters are too afraid of the night and lay curled in sleep safely down there in the village."

Clouds with bursts of light bloomed on the far slope of Atitlan.

"Bastante lluvia," said Otto. Lots of rain.

We ran toward the clouds, curving around Toliman into heavy forest as thunder rumbled. Soon, rain gushed down through the tree canopy and turned the steepening trail vicious with streams of volcanic mud. We started slipping and falling and cursing, but we didn't slow nor stop for six hours until even these hard men of the mountain needed rest. I collapsed on top of a bush, unconscious to the steady rain upon my worn self.

"Arriba," someone whispered in my ear. It was near dawn. Time to move on. I coughed. He hushed me. I coughed.

Now was the hard part, when cramps and deep pain squeezed like a skeleton's fingers and somehow we had to work through it on the fly. The camp is far away, they said. We must hurry.

No wonder they are safe up here. The army is too smart to face both this and the risk of ambush.

Hour after hour. Fall after fall. Pain upon pain.

"Hurry," said the one behind me.

I coughed.

"Hush," said the one in front who turned with his finger to his lips.

Cough.

More hours as the morning became an afternoon full of lightning bolts crashing into the woods around us. They helped take my mind away from the pain until at some point I didn't care anymore. Now, amid the lightning and rain and thunder and pain, we were streaking downhill as the trail narrowed and was more greasy as gravity pulled us faster than our feet could run. We stumbled, took headers, and I kept slipping off into the bush.

"Cuidado - minas!"

Christ, we were running through a minefield, but when I slowed down they all disappeared ahead of me in the bush. Panicked, I sped up and flew off the trail again.

"Minas!"

I don't give a shit. Let them blow me the hell out of this pain.

I almost tripped over a gun barrel sticking out of bushes. It was a machine gun implacement manned by guerrillas who expected us and didn't shoot. They grinned. Dangling vines and thorny Ceiba trees joined in the torture, ripping our clothes and puncturing our skin. Ambrose tripped on a vine and said it was like getting his foot caught in a stirrup. The trail steepened. We were almost free-falling under the influence of gravity through a field of whomping willows, or so it seemed, no longer cringing at explosions of light and bombs of noise. We gave up fear long ago and could care less if a soldier suddenly thrust his bayonet at us for we have felt so many stabs by now, and I growled to myself. "Fuck this shit! Fuckit, fuckit, fu..."

And it ended.

We burst into a grotto filled with green-clad figures, some grouped around a fire to warm their hands or stir the pot hanging over it, and as we stood gasping, they looked up and smiled.

Guerrillas around campfire

In The Guerrilla Camp

Good God, it's Robin Hood's merry men and women in Sherwood Forest.

A tall, thin woman dressed not as Maid Marian but as Robin detached from the group and strode toward me, her pale face framed with glistening black hair pulled tight behind, her large dark eyes growing bigger as she got closer and stopped a foot away, staring into me intensely. She was beautiful.

"I am Ana."

I am thunderstruck.

"Take off your clothes."

Take off your clothes? Is this my lucky day?

Ana smiled at my hesitancy and assured me with a calm, silvery tone that shamed me for my first impression.

"We are all naked to each other on the mountain and have no shame. Your clothes are wet and I will dry them by the fire."

I handed Ana my clothes and stood before her, white and skinny as a bone, and mortified to the marrow.

Another figure approached.

"Welcome, I am Comandante Pancho."

Ana

He seemed six feet tall and carried himself at ease, putting us at ease with the half-smile he wore and the careful yet flowing style of his speech — not loud or stabbing but assured, and all in camp had his respect and gave it back without being obsequious. He hugged us one by one.

"Come, meet the compadres — your compadres! And eat our food and hear who we are."

Pancho took us to the fire, which, like his demeanor, was not grand but measured, giving off just enough heat and light to simmer the great, bubbling, blackened witch's pot that hung on a rough-wood pole above the flames. A sensible fire, unlike the roaring blazes I had built a lifetime ago in the Sierra to keep the bears away. Such a fire here would lure the army in, he explained, and urged us to a favored place close to the fire, its redness reflecting on our pale skin and thawing our shivers. Not hot, just right.

Across the fire, Ana held my clothes to the flames. She caught my eye and smiled.

Someone nudged me.

"She is very nice to look at, isn't she?" said a grinning compañero. "The comandante is very lucky."

The comandante's woman?

Others started drifting up to us, introducing themselves and hugging our naked bodies as they spoke of how glad they were that we had come. A ladino named Geronimo said I would share his tent, called a *champa*, during our stay. He was anxious to speak of his time as a theater manager in Philadelphia, and why he gave it up for the real-life drama of a revolutionary.

Ana brought over my steaming clothes, which I hugged for their warmth and donned for their camouflage. Then cups were handed out and we each got black beans and a dense roll of corn meal. We also got a ladle of Incaparina, a nutritional, bland gruel dispensed in third-world countries by the United Nations. It was the heart of their dietary needs, as it was for many poor Mayan women who otherwise could not squeeze enough nourishment into their suckling babies. We gobbled it.

"We eat better this night than the guerrillas ordinarily do," Pancho said. "It's because you are here. And now, something even more rare."

He reached into his leather backpack and pulled out a large bottle of Cuban rum. His usual half-smile exploded into the most shit-eating grin, and he jubilantly explained, "Castro gave it to me when I was in Cuba and I have been looking for a special occasion to share it."

Pancho rose, holding the bottle aloft, and called everyone to the fire.

"Compañeros, we must salute the good fortune of our visitors — the first journalists to make it here alive!"

Two-dozen guerrillas gathered around the fire with cups in hand, murmuring happily. Each will get a splash, Pancho said, but our guests will get much more — and he shoved a water glass in my hand.

"Oh, that's okay, Pancho."

I handed the glass back.

"I don't drink."

He laughed and wrapped my fingers around the glass with his as twenty pairs of thirsty eyes stared at me. How do I tell them I am an alcoholic who quit drinking one night four years ago when an old man — my best friend — lay drunk at my feet, pleading to let him die.

Pancho stopped tilting the bottle when I pulled the glass away.

"I don't drink."

"Of course you do," he said with a chuckle, reaching to fill my glass.

The old man had been desperate to die by the bottle and was taking me with him. But it wasn't him pulling me into the whirlpool, it was the bottle we both had a death grip on. I wanted to live... and let go. He swirled away alone. Nothing could force me to take up drinking, again, not even these armed, incredulous revolutionaries who ached to have my glass in their hands. My vow to quit was sacred and I pulled the glass away again.

Pancho's face froze.

But is this breaking your vow, Terry? This isn't a bar. You aren't giving in to old weaknesses. There is nothing in AA's 'big book' about a moment like this, a moment like no other. When will you ever again have a chance to drink Castro's rum on a volcano with a commander of guerrillas?

I pushed the glass back at Pancho.

"Fill 'er up!"

Imagine that you are a mountain climber in the Alps, swinging from mountain to mountain, yodeling with ever more joy as you bag each peak. That's where the magical rum took me as it went down rib by rib, mountain top by mountain top, building toward a climax until it reached — The Matterhorn!

Castro rum bottle

The best, and last, drink of my life.

"Salud," I gasped.

"SALUD!" They shouted back.

"Otro?" Pancho said, ready to pour.

"No."

As I slumped onto a rough log seat, warmer than I had been in two days, Pancho shared the bottle around until it was empty and led the troop in singing a guerrilla fight song,

"Guerrillero", written to honor Che Guevara. Fueled by passion and rum, they sang like thunder.

"Guerrillero, guerrillero - forward, guerrilla!

"...forward, forward

"...to conquer or die."

In chorus, they stamped their boots on the hard mud and sang of freedom.

"Libertad!

"Libertad!

"Libertad!"

I stamped my feet, too, fully roused and, like everyone else, yearning for more rum. Ana seemed to be watching me as the rum whispered that she liked me, reminded me of my hunger, urged me to conquer or die. But the time for song and rum and passion was over, Pancho suddenly said, gathering my compadres and I around the fire. It was time to talk of revolution and why we all were here on the volcano. He motioned Ana to come over so that the Spaniard could record an interview for radio. Accompanied by the night sounds of crickets and rustling leaves, Ana spoke calm and clear and soft and strong with carefully rolled r's and carefully expressed thoughts — pure silver like her voice.

"It is a very, very hard life being a guerrilla...but it is a very satisfactory life...Here in the mountains we are all equal...This is a very special time in which to live. The pueblo is very tired. It doesn't believe anything. It hopes for a solution from us.

"Our fight is to make all Guatemalans equal..."

When Ana finished minutes later, Pancho said they were here to end four centuries of the Mayan people being crushed by the Conquistadores' children.

"Nothing else but revolution can finally stop the Conquest. It is why all our compañeros have come up the mountain."

Many heads nodded, one of them Ana's. I caught her glistening eye again and I, observing from my heights atop the Matterhorn, knew she was nodding at me.

"And you journalists are here to see who we are and tell our story to the world."

It was our turn to nod. I swelled with a rummy sense of mission, as Ambrose leaned over to whisper in my ear.

"I think I know what's going on."

Ambrose recalled an encounter during a different time between a different journalist and a different comandante of guerrillas. In 1957, Fidel Castro and Che, among 80 barely armed guerrillas, secretly debarked from Mexico to Cuba, where they were ambushed by the dictator's forces. The handful of survivors disappeared into the forests of the Sierra Maestre and found themselves hemmed in by the army. Desperate for help, the young firebrand knew he was doomed unless he could rally outside support, so he invited a New York Times reporter into his secret hideaway and poured his considerable charm upon him.

The resulting front page story exploded world opinion. Money, weapons and supplies poured in to support Castro's freedom fight. Volunteers flooded to join up as his columns came out of the mountains in a surge.

It worked for Castro, said Ambrose, and Pancho thinks it will work for him. His fighters are among just a few hundred sprinkled among the volcanoes and mountains — too entrenched for the army to find and crush, but too few to come out of the mountains ala Castro and win the day. If true, Pancho was counting on our words to help rally the world again to help win a revolution. How clever of him, the rum said, how important we are — the revolution hinges on what we write.

"It's time to sleep!" Pancho declared. "Tomorrow, you will learn the life of the guerrilla."

That night with Geronimo in his champa

The tent was commodious enough for two who weren't lovers, and he helped arrange my purple sleeping bag within. My wonderful Italian hiking boots came off with oofs of pain and relief. I slung my jeans away and, shivering in the wet cold, slid into the bag and pulled it to my chin as he unbuckled his holster with its pearl-handled Colt .38 and set it aside. His rough, cracked boots slid off. He carefully folded his forest-green, long-sleeve shirt and his khaki pants with zippered pockets. We settled in without words and lay there for a while, allowing the day's wildness to evaporate into a night of softly rustling leaves and choir of forest insects. We both stared straight up at the canvas.

"I haven't see my wife and three children in the six years since joining ORPA. My last message from them was two years ago."

Geronimo's broad, usually humor-flickering face was tense, and his words dropped like hail stones upon me for I had never met someone who traded family for ideals, especially the loving family he described, but there was yet another love he mused about with fondness and a rare smile — a theater of actors he had managed in Philadelphia and of his dream to do the same in Guatemala after the triumph. I almost gasped.

"Theater, Geronimo!? Hey, I love acting and my life's biggest hero is Cyrano de Bergerac for defending his ideals and the downtrodden to the death." His spirit hovers within me, I thought, and no doubt helped goad me to Guatemala the first time with idealistic notions of helping Mayans escape poverty and disease. "But, I became frustrated and knew my efforts were doomed to failure."

Gesturing to a nearby rack full of weapons, he said, "The only solution is armed revolution. There is no other way to put an end to 400 years of oppression. You must tell the world this. Tell them the truth!"

The truth? I don't know what the fucking truth is. Sadness is the truth. Fear is the truth. Death is the truth. If you are Mayan or want to help them, getting killed is the truth. If you're a soldier, killing Mayans is the truth. These are truths I've eyeballed, but... THE truth? I'm so fucking confused, and the rum isn't helping.

"I will, Gernonimo. I will."

There was more to say but more nights to say it. We drifted into silence and dead heavy sleep.

Day 2

Ahhh, a sunny morning, yet I shivered in rays dripping through the neblina. Last night, off by myself in a corner of the camp, watching the good cheer of everyone despite the rain and cold and mud of their world, I wrote: "It is wet all the time. Things never seem to dry. The rain only stops briefly. How do these people manage?" Pancho wandered over as if he had read my mind.

"How long do you think you could put up with this — a month?"

Not another day, not another moment.

"You must have a cause to put up with this, Pancho."

His eyes lighted.

"Yes, a cause..."

He pulled a brown, briar pipe from his pocket and put its black stem to his lips, chewing on it and some thoughts.

"The revolution keeps us warm through the difficult days and years up here."

Impressive to hear, but theoretical to one like me whose bones were cold for lack of cause, and I shivered almost violently as Pancho led me to the fire where Ana awaited with words of why she was here. At 29, she was the second daughter in a family of rebels except for her father — a colonel in the army — and a brother, the only chip off the old block. The three daughters and mother were fighters or collaborators. Mom, who was also an ORPA urban militant, had started Ana on the path up the mountain by having her read such books as Les Miserables, the story of young French people at the barricades, fighting to bring freedom to the masses.

How fascinating she was, especially when she revealed her education by Maryknolls. We had a connection.

Ana almost met Pancho at the University of San Carlos, but he left the year she entered and their first meeting would have wait. She stayed to earn a degree in agronomy and tried to revolutionize the lives of campesinos without picking up arms.

"I lived a fine life and liked fine things until I went into the countryside as a student to help the Mayan people live better lives and discovered that the government was using people like me to keep the indigenous people bound in their old lives. We weren't helping the people, we were helping the government control the people."

She tried to improve farming but just as I saw in Cunén, the parcels were too small and shitty, the seeds and fertilizer too expensive. "How can you help when all you are doing is showing them impossible ways to succeed?" she said. I hadn't thought of it that way. I always saw my aid group as doing a kind of God's work by healing wounds and helping people to endure tough lives. Not once did I see them as Ana did, as permanent pawns in an ancient con game.

"When we tried to achieve agrarian reform — to put more and better land into their hands — we were accused of being communists." And suspected communists were murdered. All around her, students and friends and teachers were victims of this holocaust. Any attempts to organize to build better lives were brutally quashed. She was shocked to see USAID funds, earmarked to provide contraceptives, instead being used in sterilization programs to keep the native population from growing. Other AID funds for housing were channeled into building the concentration camps we had seen in Nebaj. And that was just the start of Ana's political autopsy — spoken without leftist rhetoric — of how the U.S. was helping crush the Mayan world.

"We are like servants of the U.S....like Czechoslovakia and Hungary are to Russia."

Ana saw no choice. Passivity would save her but then she would be complicit in the slaughter of others. She went up the mountain four years ago and, "I have had no contact with my family or friends since." The brief sad shadow across her face was replaced by firmness in her jaw and voice.

"How long will you stay?"

"Until the triumph. Ni un paso atras - not one step back." So familiar her words, echoing those of another civil war leader, Abraham Lincoln: "I never walk backwards."

I was mesmerized as she spoke and Pancho watched.

"How has it been...up here?" I asked.

"Once I was a firebrand but four years of combat and life in the mountains have changed me." Made her cooler, more thoughtful, and sadder. She spoke with a gentle, fine, quiet lilt. Her face was delicate, her hands eloquent in their gestures. She was pretty, despite the rough green uniform. She seemed weary.

To the bone. Yet she could perk up at a jest or bright memory and show a bit of gaiety. And she was clearly Pancho's woman, although no such words of bondage seemed appropriate here on the mountain where every man and woman saw themselves as free agents. She rebelled when Ambrose asked if she was a feminist.

"The guerrilla movement is the same as the womans movement. I don't fight a feminist cause...my cause is of a country in chains."

"Chains with many links forged by Ronald Reagan," Pancho said. "He is pouring aid into the hands of generals to destroy us."

That fucking Reagan. Haven't liked him since I interviewed him as a college journalist when he ran for governor. Full of dreamy platitudes about killing evil communists to make the world safe for democracy. My farm town was full of billboards declaring this as "Reagan Country." But this down here is the real Reagan country. Awash with his donations of advisors, equipment, weapons and political support for a murderous regime.

"We will win the revolution, but not until Reagan is gone," Pancho said, and I wondered if he could endure four more years. He had already been here six years, since he was 26, the same age I was when running on the road to Nebaj in 1973, looking with happy awe at broiling, lightning-filled clouds atop these volcanoes.

"We will win because we treat all people equally and they support us," Ana said.

Pancho then spoke to a different angle on equality.

"Everyone is equal on the mountain, even when it comes to sex, as long as there is a mutual accord. We have never had a rape. If a woman wants sex she may have it with whoever – it never creates trouble. There are some homosexuals, but that's OK as long as they are good brave fighters."

The sex discussion left me uneasy.

Pancho turned to Geronimo and a different subject.

"Show Terry your specialty."

Geronino smiled in a humor-soaked way that flavored him and led me to a place in the forest where he made mines. Like a proud pie maker, he showed me one of his wares — a small one with only five pounds of explosives. It was gray as a corpse, thick as an unabridged dictionary, and wide as a dinner plate, concave on one side where two electrical wires emerged to be connected to a detonator. He made it of pine sap warmed to flow into a mold around a circle of wire with the explosive in the middle.

"We can make six mines a day and some of them are as large as 30 kg — powerful enough to kill an entire patrol," he said proudly. The mine is connected to a detonating device held by a guerrilla hidden just off the trail in a *matapolo*, a kind of malicious growth that takes over a pine tree like a snake swallowing prey and sucks its life out, leaving a rotted opening in its trunk. To the guerrilla, matapolo was a perfect metaphor for what the government was doing to the people, and it was soothing for one of them to sit within such a tree, waiting for soldiers to sneak within range of a mine planted along the trail.

"We have a warning system," Geronimo said, pointing upwards to the tree canopy where wild turkeys, parrots and many other species of birds created a constant background din in various bird lingos. "The forest tells us when our enemies approach."

When the birds suddenly shriek with a single voice: "Boom."

I was even more chilled after our talk, and declined his suggestion to plunge into a river where various compañeros, including Ana, were bathing naked.

"Too cold," I said, but the real reason was, I would stare at her. The guerrilla Tito understood. He hadn't stopped looking at her from the moment she first came to camp in 1981.

She came in the middle of the night.

"What is an angel doing here?" he thought when he awoke in the morning and saw a tall, fair-skinned woman whose thinness made her large eyes look enormous. "She appeared too delicate. All the other women were Mayan, built close to the ground with stout legs and muscular buttocks perfect for carrying heavy loads in rough terrain. Everything about the camp was difficult — the terrain, the weather, the food, the ground we slept on."

So fragile and yet she carried a heavy backpack. "The weight doesn't matter," she said. "I will always carry my own weight."

She was very shy. There were so many men, all carrying arms.

"I mean, what the fuck was she doing here?"

The answer came from her own lips when Pancho introduced her to the camp.

"I have come up the mountain to be one of you, and I will not take one step backwards — *ni un paso atras* — until the revolution is won."

Ana was no diplomat, Tito quickly discovered. She spoke like she fought. Direct, straight from the shoulder. He learned about her fearlessness when she insisted on joining an attack on soldiers at a farm.

"At around 3 a.m. we were silently walking the farm road, looking for the army. Ana said she would go ahead. I said no, but she kept going and after a bit told everyone to sit for she had seen a guard at the farmhouse. We stayed quiet about five minutes watching the soldier come in and out of the house. He was just talking. We shot a rocket into the house, which exploded - killing 20 soldiers.

"She was no bullshit."

But she did seduce the poet in Tito, an ascetic-thin fellow with a sharp-edged face, a soft heart and a bubbling soul. He had a lover's passion for the revolution, for their cause, for the Mayans they fought for, and for Ana.

Often, he watched her sitting at river's edge, where a willow tree bent into the current, its thin branches softly bobbing as its leaves danced in the flow. He was fascinated by her ritual of plucking a cigarette from a pack on a rock. She would light the cigarette and trace the air with its smoke as she sat staring with her big eyes. She did not appear to see anything outward. Her view was inward, he said, where a river of thoughts swirled. She was so full of thoughts — about the revolution, about the camp, about fighting, about humanity and equality and so many other things. Tito believed it was here where she assembled her teachings and inspirations for the compañeros and, ultimately, for the Mayan people of the village Santiago Atititlan at the base of the volcano. She was in charge of protecting and educating the village.

"You loved her?"

Tito and Ana in camp

"Yes," he said, his voice trailing off, his eyes staring off...a love from afar.

I, too, was affected — by the beauty in how she talked and thought, the excitement she showed when describing battles with the army, the way her face lit up at a dear memory, and the unutterable depths of sadness when she spoke of lost comrades and of the Mayan people at the heart of her cause. Like Tito, I watched her with my heart, and it didn't go unnoticed.

"Come, compañeros, let us have a bottle dance," Pancho announced that night.

A bottle dance?

"Si."

He pulled from his knapsack the emptied bottle of rum that Castro gave him.

"This is the bottle," he said, holding it out at eye level and moving it around for all to see.

"It represents something of great value. We dance to win it."

He bent to place the bottle in the center of the packed mud floor, away from the cooking fire. The compañeros formed a circle about 15 feet across, grinning and jostling each other. We three journalists stood with Pancho near the bottle as he turned his head from left to right, looking into our eyes and smiling his own slight grin.

"Who wants the bottle?"

He looked at me.

"Terry?"

Hah! I liked this and grinned back at him, nodding my head with vigor

The compañeros liked it, too, and trilled the r's of my name..."Ter-r-r-y."

Pancho demonstrated how the dance was done: hands grasped behind his body as he stomped the dirt rhythmically with his feet, circling the bottle, turning his shoulders left with a foot stomp and right with another stomp. Halfway around he sprung over the bottle with a shout and landed with a double stomp that his compadres cheered.

"How do we know who the winner is?" I asked.

The compañeros laughed.

"The winner? The winner is the one left standing."

And now I realized that the two of us dance at the same time. That we circle the bottle with our feet pawing like a bull's hooves. That we launch ourselves over the bottle and into each other. That we keep it up until one of us has been knocked down.

"We call the bottle 'the woman.' "

A woman! In this circle of celibates, what could be more yearned for?

Pancho turned to his compadres and started clapping a rhythm: one-two-three, one-two-three, one-two-three, ONE! They picked up the clap as Pancho dropped his hands behind him and started dancing around the bottle, stomping to each clap, stomping with extra force on the ONE! I joined in across the bottle from him and started my dance.

One-two-three,

One-two-three,

One-two-three,

ONE!

We circled the bottle, eyeing each other with our heads still and our shoulders snapping left and right to the beat.

One-two-three,

One-two-

Pancho leaped at me over the bottle with his left shoulder forward and I barely had time to spin, leave my feet, and repel him with my right shoulder. We jolted off each other, laughing. The stomping and stalking renewed as the companeros laughed and the clapping sped up.

One-two-three,

One-two-three,

One-

I ambushed Pancho by leaping with my left shoulder! The collision jarred me. Pancho was a man of muscle.

One-two-three,

One-two-three,

A counterattack from Pancho! I fell back with the sting of his fierceness on my shoulder.

Warily, this time, our dance resumed within a circle that had tightened as compañeros leaned in and murmured to the beating of their hands and the pounding of our feet.

Left shoulder,

Right shoulder,

One-two-three,

SLAM!

The play was knocked out of me, and now as I circled, my eyes glanced away from Pancho's and into the eyes of the guerrillas. Every eye flickered in the light of our campfire. My eyes paused in the wide-open eyes of the tallest. Ana.

ONE!

The hardest blow, yet, from Pancho.

Good God, is this about Ana? Is she the woman of the bottle?

Fool! All you have done since coming to this camp is stare at Ana as if she were a bikini-clad girl at Newport Beach or a steak or the girl I left behind. Ana, who dresses like Castro, but doesn't shout her ideals to the masses. She flows them out with bright soft clarity as if she was talking just to you. And looks steadily at you as she talks. You are not used to such a woman, whose eyes seek not to seduce but to connect. Whose voice has no trickery in its softness.

Whose words aren't for you but for the world. A world that she wants to awaken to the plight of people who have been enslaved by their country's landlords.

The flickers I had been seeing in each eye were becoming flames in my imagination as the dance intensified. The ground shook because the compadres were stomping, too, and clapped quicker, as Pancho and I swirled faster and bashed into each other harder over the empty bottle.

Too intense.

A thought ... Of a short story called "The Devil and Daniel Webster." About some damned farmer in the time just before our own Civil War who got rich by selling his soul to the devil and now the devil has come to collect. The farmer had hired the famous lawyer to defend him with fierce self-righteousness before a jury and judge from Hell.

"But ... he noticed the glitter in their eyes was twice as strong as before, and they all leaned forward. Like hounds just before they get the fox...Then he saw what he'd been about to do, and he wiped his forehead, as a man might who's just escaped falling into a pit in the dark."

Fire against fire didn't work for Daniel and it was not working for Terry.

Pancho rattled me with another blow.

What have I brought with me into this enclave of equals? Something they left behind when they came up the steep path to be as one in a struggle for all. They are idealists who aren't just fighting for what they believe; they are living it. I felt profane all of a sudden.

And anxious.

Pancho wasn't fooling around. And his compañeros weren't singing Kumbaya.

I had to make this a game again, where the prize is a bottle and not a woman. An empty bottle.

It was time to lose.

"Whoa!" I shouted with a laugh as I stumbled at the next encounter.

Clapping like a Flamenco dancer with my hands overhead, I whooped to the beat and jumped chest first into Pancho's shoulder and caromed to the ground, rolling to the feet of the guerrillas. Who were laughing.

"Muy bien!" Pancho declared with a smile and helped me to my feet.

We embraced.

And I no longer gazed so openly at...his woman.

That night in the champa
with Geronimo

"I hate killing. I hate killing. I hate killing....but if you don't kill them they kill you and many more than you — they kill the people. That is why we fight! I have killed many."

Moments passed as heavy rain splattered the tent. He sighed deeply.

"Ahhh, Terry, I don't like killing."

Day 3

How could it be that here, surrounded by coffee plantations, we don't have coffee for breakfast? I'm not grumpy, just curious.

"Cups of coffee don't grow on trees - just beans," Pancho explained as we gnawed cold tamales in the morning drizzle. "Beans must be processed down there, in Santiago, and the coffee brought up here on someone's back. Everything comes on someone's back. Food, weapons, bullets…"

Food talk reignited food fantasies I dreamed last night after a sparse dinner of hard tamales and Incaparina. "Everyone dreams of food," he said, "but tonight we all will dream with sonrisas — smiles."

He stood to welcome three companeros returning to camp with an entire cow's haunch, its leg and hoof sticking out over one compañero's back with the heavy muscled hip balanced on his shoulder, still bleeding where machetes had hacked it off. The trio grinned like clowns as they trotted toward the fire. My belly rumbled.

"We paid the farmer for his cow," Pancho assured me, just as they pay for all of the food local farmers provide. Most of the farmers are friendly to them…most, but not all. Last night I got into a terse exchange with him when a patrol of guerrilleros returned after failing to find and kill an "oreja" — a campesino suspected of being a spy.

"How could you just kill someone like that as if you were judge and jury," I asked with a twinge of indignation. "Killing peasants is what the EGP did up in Nebaj."

He shifted on his seat.

"In war you kill to stay alive. Many of us would die if a spy led the army here. And we are not the EGP, which made many mistakes in how they treated the people. We are careful and sensible. Even the army might tell you that about us."

Sensible...like Father Kavanaugh said. And yet, talk like this leaves me colder than the neblina. I don't understand killing. It is as theoretical to me as how their ideals keep them warm and dedicated and away from families and comfort year after year in these cold, damp, dangerous climes.

"Except when we fight the army, our work is not about killing," he emphasized.

To him, ORPA was like an armed labor union, often policing the fincas for signs of worker abuse. They forced finca owners at the point of a gun to open their books to show what they pay laborers. "A warning is given: we'll be back to burn you out if things don't improve. As a result — and because we don't put the people between us and the army — we enjoy broad popular support. Because of that we believe the ultimate triumph is possible."

But there is more to it than that, Ana said.

"The ultimate triumph willl also come when the Mayan people see themselves as equals within a society that gives them the same life opportunities as us." By us, she meant the mixed-blood/white-skin people whose natural confidence in their own equality is more than skin deep. "We are who we are because we were raised in that belief and live confidently without even thinking about it."

Almost on cue, visitors from Santiago arrived, three campesinos wearing masks to prevent being identified. The army has killed more of us in the village, they said.

One them, a father of seven, spoke bitterly of paying bribes and ransom money to free his 25-year-old son from jail after the army seized him. But the army kept the kid and demanded more money.

The second man's father was arrested by the army "for no reason." He, too, has paid considerable money, yet his father has not been freed.

They feared that their son and father were dead like 300 others "disappeared" from the village by the army in the last four years.

So what do they expect Pancho and his force to do — go down there in the middle of the night to attack the army and try to free their brethren or take vengeance? They don't ask. He gives no sense of outrage, but exudes empathy. His response makes sense to me in light of how often he and Ana spoke of being careful not to repeat the mistakes made by the guerrillas of the Nebaj area whose violent acts lacked strategic purpose and put the people between them and the red hats.

The third fellow, only 18, begged Pancho to let him join so that he could fight for better things in life like decent food and freedom from fear. He feared becoming one of the disappeared like so many he knows. "Think it over for five days.

Then come back," Pancho said. Too much of a 'beardless young man,' I guessed.

When the campesinos left, a very young, energy-bursting compañera named Lidia insisted on talking with us. She was 17, Mayan and full of the moral outrage described by the firebrand Ana until years of brutish reality tempered her.

"We are hungry. We are exploited. We are miserable. We want to live like you do in the way of humans — with liberty and equality."

She described the work on fincas as pure exploitation. Poor food. Long, hard work. Poor pay. "We are forced to do the work while the rich ones get everything." She lowered her voice to a hard hiss when she uttered "rich ones."

"They are gorged with food. They are fat from drinking the blood of the people. We don't want to live as animals, as garbage anymore. We slave for them and what do we get — torture, massacre, and neglect!"

She was so filled with fury, spitting out her words with the staccato of a machine gun. Her words filled six pages of my notebook, and there were many more I wasn't fast enough to catch.

"We are in the guerrilla because it is the only way. Yes, it is hard, but we are fighting to make it easier."

With all her memorized phrases and fast talk, Lidia sounded like what Ambrose called "coffee shop leftists" except that she was here amid the coffee fields where coffee itself is a luxury, dressed in green, armed, living the hard life, going on patrols, throwing herself into battle. Giving up her youth and maybe her life for the cause that kept them all warm here in the constant cold and wet. The cause to create a country they don't have to flee.

"Come," Geronimo broke in. "It's time for our political education session."

Lidia and a dozen other guerrilleros grouped around him as he read from ORPA's mimeographed newspaper, "The Words of the Pueblo." Not everyone could read, which is why both he and Ana taught rudimentary reading and writing, using political material such as this. Today's lesson was about the upcoming elections and why it doesn't matter who wins because the army runs the country. It seemed like old news to them. They'd rather fight than listen. They slapped mosquitoes, shuffled feet, glanced around, but Gernonimo called each by name and demanded that they repeat what he said. This is life, not high school, and no one was allowed to fail.

Ana said she has been going down into Santiago, teaching the Mayan residents these same things. More importantly, she was teaching them the concept of equality: to believe they are as good as anyone on the planet. "Somos iguales — we are all equal," she said, pausing as I pondered how much like Thomas Jefferson she sounded, as if she was channeling the flourish of his hand as he inked the heart of our Declaration of Independence: "All men are created equal." To believe that no rich person, no white person, no ladino, no norteamericano was better by reason of birth. And, in a special message to women, she reenforced the idea of equality with men. "You are not born to do their bidding." Ana was teaching them to look within and see how they had been all their lives and their ancestors all their lives — taught to believe they were less (Indian shit, the Kaibil had said) because they were Mayan *and* women.

This last part almost made my legs weak. She was talking to them like my mother used to talk out loud to herself. Saying the same thing over and over. *No one is better than you, No one is better than you, No one…*Saying it over and over until one day she marched out of her house full of seven, hungry children to compete in the male world her husband could not. Saying it to her dreamy, fearful second son who ran from bullies. *No one is better than you, Terry, No one is better than you.* Saying it over and over until I started saying it to myself and stopped running.

"The revolution will be won up here," Pancho interjected, pointing to his head. "Not boom, boom with this," pointing to his rifle.

Thunder suddenly cracked close by, sounding like a large tin sheet being shaken.

Pancho pulled us away so that he could list his front's recent "accomplishments." Lots of work among the fincas, forcing owners and overseers to open heir books — one in particular, a large coffee and cattle operation called "Moca Grande." Aside from the usual forced servitude of campesinos and horrid pay, the finca had a torture center in the owner's house, protected by 150 soldiers. He asked us to warn authorities about this fellow — that ORPA will kill him if this continues. In a few weeks, I would regret mentioning it to a grim man in Guatemala City.

Pancho was most proud of shooting down an army helicopter on the slopes of Volcano Toliman three years before.

Decades later I read in army chronicles about how survivors of the crash, hidden in thick bush, heard Pancho order his fighters not to kill any of them.

He emphasized how important it was to let the world know about these successes and their continuing fight.

"The people need to know that our revolution thrives among the volcanoes and our values are the values of Guatemalans, not Nicaragua or Cuba or Russia. We are not murderers or terrorists or communists.

"We are not fanatics but hard men and women fighting a war for the people."

"What is Russia like?" a young compañera asked me abruptly.

"Never been there, but I hear it's tough for most people who live under the control of a few in a system that forces all to work in collectives. They don't allow private businesses."

"And America?"

"People have jobs, nice homes, cars, good food..."

"I want to go to America."

How could you blame him?

What kind of system would the guerrillas like to see in Guatemala?

Otto laid out ORPA's official five-point plan, filled with glittering hopes such as making a society that ends repression and guarantees dignity for all.

"The revolution will work to assure all the population fundamental necessities, and end economic and political domination by the great, rich exploiters and end repression by nationals and foreigners. The revolution will bring good things, will end killings, arrests, will bring good food. Children will have better lives."

What the plan didn't do was offer a plan. Ambrose picked up on its glittering, substance-free message when he later wrote:

"But the sad truth is that few of my fine friends, if any, would have much say in the revolutionary junta. Some wretched communist would come to the fore and ruin everything; some vile ideologue would steal the revolution from the peasants who wrought it." Exactly what happened with Nicaragua's revolt.

The plan offered brave hopes but not much to chew on, unlike that night's feast on the cow haunch which drizzled juices as it cooked over the fire, popping and sizzling until our mouths dripped with desire. We were given plates of beef first but could not gulp them faster than the compañeros who ripped long strings of smoky, blooded beef that, I swear, disappeared down some throats without being chewed. One fellow turned his head upwards like he was swallowing a sword. Zuuup! Down it went. Others gnawed and gulped as hungry dogs. There even were bits of unsweetened chocolate and coffee! A feast to tell stories about ages hence.

And then came dessert, a guerrilla theater directed, of course, by Geronimo who played the lead role of then-President Mejia Victores holding above his head a bloody bone from the just-devoured cow. It was labeled, 'PresidenCIA'. Three guerrillas labeled with the names of the three political parties groveled at his feet, snapping and whining for bits of flesh. The scene hearkened a Guatemalan saying: *"Peleándose el hueso"* - fighting over the bone (power).

Three other actors — one wearing my blue cowboy hat with its colorful ribbon from Nebaj — played roles as international bankers demanding payment of the country's debt. The "president" shrugged and turned his pockets inside out. "No dinero." So, they told him to quit wasting money on workers. Good idea, he said, and poured them all drinks representing money diverted from the people to them. "Sabroso," he declared, smacking his lips after drinking "the blood of the people."

———

That night in the champa
with Geronimo

"What do you think of the guerrillas, Terry?"

"I only know your group, Geronimo, and what I know of it is good. But how can you win?"

"By faith, by perseverance. Because our cause is right."

Idealism and bullets, but, can they win against the most vicious army in Latin America? Too tough a question. Instead, I asked, "What is the guerrillas' greatest desire?"

"Ice cream."

We both slept on that thought.

Day 4

Finally, on this fourth morning, the cold was only skin deep and I shivered, not shook, in the wet hug of the neblina as I balanced on one foot outside the champa, while jamming the other into my mud-blue jeans.

"Ter-r-r-y," a companero said softly as he strolled by with his rifle slung across his back and disappeared into the misty forest.

"He's going on patrol."

Pancho's sudden voice startled me and we both laughed as my pants dropped around my ankles. He had a steaming mug of — I squinted into it — not coffee, goddammit. Incaparina. But it was warm and I grabbed it after buckling my pants. The belt needed an extra hole to stay tight. The fire was warm, too, though it had no flames nor even smoke. They kept it discreet in daylight to avoid giving off even the slightest tendril of smoke that an army patrol could zero in on. The witch's pot, of course, hung over the coals. Other compañeros stood around the fire as we came to it. This was their stove, in their kitchen, just as if we were down there in a proper home where family members and friends gather to eat and talk about how they slept and what their plans were for the day and how this body part ached and so on. They dipped into the pot and warmed their hands on its vapors. It was all rounded like the fat belly of Buddha and had something of a lip around its top where its metal hoop handle was hooked to both sides. Coming or going, the compañeros always passed this wondrous object and sometimes paused as if in prayer or in hopes it would bubble out something delicious. Pancho said it was as important as any weapon. Food is life. In an army ambush that almost cost all their lives, they had to decide whether to leave the heavy, bulky, noisy pot or risk taking it as they crawled through army lines. There was no question, Pancho wrote. Food is life.

As I sipped gruel, the sun was weaving the neblina into translucent lace that caressed Pancho and I as we strolled through the rain forest.

"This is our garden of Eden," he said, talking of how he had come to love this high homeland full of wild creatures, fantastic plants and dark crevices in the earth that aren't just great places for an ambush but sanctuaries for the soul. I didn't have my notebook to record his unexpectedly poetic thoughts, but the book he wrote years later captured everything and more of what we talked about, and it hinted that Pancho might never have seen nor felt this spiritual connection to the natural world if not for someone he met before coming up the mountain. Her name was Gabriela. And, like Ana, she had an entire chapter in his book devoted to her.

She was like the dawn to him, a cultured woman who helped him grow and value himself, and to recognize, respect, and love nature. She opened his eyes to wonders within the mountain's crevices where he had only seen places to hide and ambush — the contradiction of beauty that obscures the danger that blinds us to beauty. There are wild things to marvel at, she said, like the jacaranda, a lavender flower shaped like a pitcher that lures you close with its fragrance and makes you want to pour yourself within... the feeling I had experienced when first looking into Ana's eyes. He credits Gabriela with awakening his eyes and soul so that he could write: "One can not imagine the depth and extraordinary beauty that the Sierra Madre hides in its entrails."

At first, those entrails — the deep forested *barrancas* (canyons) — appeared threatening and impossible to penetrate. But the dangers of war gave him no choice. Like an armed foe, you must face up to it and keep going until your fear is transformed "into a true love...She was...Our house. Our mother. We were entering the draped velvet of her skirts. Her beauty is dazzling, more than any nomad could imagine. Its fantastic plant variety, from the immense trees of the area closest to the coast... to the thousand-year-old conifers that rock at their heights and that have no arboreal forms but reptilian as they crawl to defend themselves against the wind that breaks loose next to the crater of the volcano — it made us see a green sea that gave us protection against infantry and aviation."

Here on its slopes, he wrote, were born many rivers that flowed to the sea and were in fact the corridors we three journalists would use for our escape. How sad that we had no Gabriela to teach us about the snakes, coatis, herds of wild pigs, and deer large as cows or small and speckled and tame because they had never seen a human and hadn't learned to fear. There was so much life up here. As Pancho described:

"The roar of the puma at night, marking its territory invaded by the guerrilla camp. The monkeys moving through the branches like a guerrilla column. All this was a prelude to the culminating moment in the life of the mountain: the appearance of the quetzal. It was as if God had made the arbors, the clouds, the springs for his flight."

The quetzal — fantastically beautiful with green tail plumage that flows down like an iridescent waterfall — can only be seen in the most remote, high, thickly forested places where war forced Pancho to go. It is the country's national bird and to the indigenous people, he wrote, is their sacred Gucumatz, the serpent bird. The Spaniards didn't believe it existed, but then they were seeking a different gold and didn't have a Gabriela to open their eyes. In April and May, Pancho wrote, the quetzals were everywhere up there.

"Eight to ten pairs of quetzals in the same tree, celebrating the rite of love. I speak of the quetzal but there is another, the guardabarranco — a small, gray and ugly little bird who wakes us with his first trills in the morning. His song rises from the depths of the ravine... the most beautiful sound of the mountain."

He was sure that none of this beauty and magic would have been visible to him if not for Gabriela.

"I love her," he told himself on the last day they were together in 1979, just before he went up the mountain. Her last words to him were a warning: "It is good that you are going up the mountain for they are going to kill us."

Two years later, in the months when the army began its most bloody and vengeful attacks throughout the country,

Pancho went down into the city and was driving with a compañero along what he called a sinister street when he saw Gabriela walking in their direction: "I saw her so withered, wrinkled and with the sad look, she was floating, her feet no longer impacted against the pavement, she was lost, out of this world. Not at all the beautiful and sensual woman I knew."

Behind Gabriela, a vehicle crept. It was white with tinted glass, the kind used by army kidnappers and death squads, and feared by all; a hearse for the living whose door was slightly open to allow quick grabbing or quicker shooting.

"With her hands, with a gesture or a whisper she could have given us death ... but she passed by our side indifferently and continued. I smiled at her. She evaded the look so that they would not kill me, and she continued straight ahead... towards eternity, from where she never returned, and where nothing was ever heard of her, like another Guatemalan disappeared. I never heard from her again...I never saw the jacarandas again in her eyes, but in the absolute vegetation of the mountain, in the thickest of the combats, I continued listening to her kind voice. Gabriela — flower and cinnamon, aroma and sweetness, hardness and bitterness, the seed of war."

Pancho fled back up the mountain, where soon, in the middle of one night, Ana walked into his life. And like Tito and me, he was smitten. So physically beautiful. So brave — in a way that any man could admire. She spoke not of flowers but of a flowering cause and her yearning to start fighting for it. Her chance came soon in an attack she led against the elite Kaibiles on the flanks of a volcano south of Atitlan. The guerrillas were pinned down by Kaibiles spraying them with a heavy machine gun that dropped a number of them. Ana stood and directed a rocket launch that pierced the heart of enemy defenses. A fighter begged that she take care.

"Ana, let's retreat, you cannot expose yourself this way. You are the leader."

She snapped, "Haroldo, what you have is fear. We all shake with it."

Capitan Hernan — the grinning guerrilla next to Ana in the photo on Pancho's wall — grinned again 30 years later as he recalled how calm and even light-hearted she seemed in that moment when the army had surrounded them and they all feared for their lives. "The tiger hair pops when it is about to attack — and hers had risen." In the photo she is looking around, happy by appearance. She was calming them all, giving them strength for whatever may come. It was infectious. Perhaps the soldiers felt it for they retreated.

There were other such fights that made the compañeros respect and trust her, one in particular when her courage and calm sustained even the commander. The troop was again surrounded by the army — the worst position for any guerrilla to face. In the middle of the night they crawled through the army lines so close to soldiers they could see their boots and feel them touch the earth. Pancho was unnerved. The army had occupied the camp they just fled.

"We saw so many campfires in the army that I thought it was an impossible feat to have escaped unharmed. In a state of extreme physical and mental insanity, I told her, 'I cannot anymore, I already feel that the helicopters are crawling on the earth, I have lost the dimension of time and space.'

"She took me in her lap, hugged me and told me something that is still a balm: "Sleep. I'm going to take care of you.""

Pancho and I continued walking the forest trail that morning as he described the breadth of ORPA's territory, ranging south to the flanks of Volcan Agua and north beyond the highest point in Central America — the grand volcano Tajamulco. They traveled among these high peaks and sweeping slopes, openly at night on trails and during the day by canyons — the guerrilla subway — where the army was loath to penetrate.

Tito recalled one such passage when they encountered an army patrol and a young, female guerrilla leaped from tree to tree like a monkey, shooting, leaping, shooting. Playing peek-a-boo with bullets.

That night in the champa
with Geronimo

Geronimo again lay awake, talking softly.

"What makes a good guerrilla is what makes a person brave — the willingness to trade one's personal interests for those of the pueblo. Do you understand why I spend so much time in 'indoctrination' sessions with the young fighters?"

No.

"So that they know why they are fighting. To know why is to be brave.""

The words I overheard him telling his fighters made me twist in my purple sleeping bag. They spoke of the harm my country had brought to his country through its support of the army they were fighting. We supplied the bombs, the planes that dropped the bombs, and the helicopters that constantly flew over searching for them, the enemy. We underwrote a system that takes their land and labor, and steals their future. My country. Me?

Day 5

It is time for war games on this, our last full day in camp. Geronimo has already educated me about the difference in training between guerrillas and soldiers. A soldier in the Guatemalan army trains openly without fear and may shoot thousands of rounds of ammunition learning how to accurately take down a foe. The guerrilla has no such pleasure. Training is done where the fighting is done, among the trails and thickets of forest, and not a single bullet is shot for practice. They have so few, all purchased on the black market or stolen from dead soldiers and hauled up the mountain like coffee on campesinos' backs. The fear of being caught is far greater than the physical burden. In a year, the entire front might shoot 150 bullets in battle, a fraction of that sprayed at them by soldiers in a single fight.

A training exercise conducted as a demonstration for us seemed almost comical. A dozen or so guerrillas went up the trail and hid along it waiting in ambush while we three journalists were the army patrol led by a pretend army leader who announced that our job was to kill terrorists and drink their blood. It was hard to keep a straight face as we went single file down the trail as if we were soldiers, and I almost laughed when suddenly we heard "Pah, Pah" from the bush as hidden guerrillas shot us dead with bursts of breath.

"Boom," said someone. A mine.

"You are surrounded," Pancho said. "You are dead." He was serious. They were serious. I throttled a grin as if it were a cough.

Eighty or so times his front has ambushed the army like this, causing up to 40 deaths at a time, Pancho said.

As I read my old notebook, I remembered what Pancho had written of ambushes in his memoir: "The ambush is the sanctum sanctorum of the guerrilla... the culminating moment when...the small and the weak concentrate all their power to hit the strongest." Aside from being practical, the ambush reflects the contrast between Western ideals of honor and war, and Oriental/guerrilla concepts. One believes in lines of combatants attacking head-on in full force. The other is like the neblina itself — there and not there.

"In an eternal turning on itself and the enemy, the ambush is precisely that: to evade and deceive the enemy and strike it surprisingly and in the time where it least expects it... and it must strike down as if the wrath of God."

Patience is the secret to a good ambush. It is harsh to lie in the bush by the side of the path for endless hours in the dark and light and rain and neblina. To shiver with cold and ache with hunger. To keep your focus as time and ordinary people pass by oblivious to the danger that is not theirs, some chatting frivolously, some staggering in the aftermath of partying, and here come torch-carrying family members like ghosts. So boring that as you chew stale beans and share disconsolate glances with your compañeros lying near you, there is a danger that your eyes may sleep and miss the "slow-motion movie" of the first soldier leading many more.

"They walk exhausted and hungry, giving the impression that they do not care about anything that happens around them. Ignorant and even contemptuous of the possibility of their death. It is an image that hits you like an electric current. The entrance route to the death zone."

There is a strange communication "beyond the senses" between those who are going to kill and those who are going to die. In a small country like Guatemala where almost everyone knows or has seen each other, you may discover a few meters from the Claymore mine the eyes of an officer that was your acquaintance in adolescence, you can see that he, too, at the last moment sees you and recognizes you... the mine explodes and the soldier's body is impelled to the heights like a sheet of paper that begins to be written in red."

Many of their tactics were outlined by Che Guevara in his writings, Pancho said.

"Do you know about Che?"

I was too embarrassed to tell him. In 1966, the year I was rejected by the army draft, I was a volunteer at a Mexican-American help center in deeply right-wing Orange County, California. Like the other earnest, white volunteers, we didn't know shit about things south of the border except that Castro was stirring revolution in the "banana republics," whatever they were. The Russians were behind it and maybe the Chinese — like in Viet Nam where we were holding the line on communism. Thank God, we thought, that Che who after helping Castro win Cuba for the commies, had been killed before he could light communist revolutions throughout the Americas. Someone at the Center had an idea for raising money by sponsoring and promoting the first film at a new theater about to open. In return, we would get opening night proceeds. I jumped on the idea without knowing what film it was, signed the contract, and a few days later reeled in shock.

The film was, "Che!" starring Omar Shariff. The others freaked, but I went straight to The Orange County Register — one of the rightist-wing papers in America — to get publicity as I had for my other promotions. They practically threw me out. No publicity for that communist son of a bitch! Hence, when the movie opened, the theater was only half full, mostly with invited members from the Mexican-American community who sat in the front row as the movie began with ear-popping explosions and machine gun fire and the announcer screaming 'CHE!' It was nothing but blood and guts and killing and lurid descriptions of Che as a communist killing machine. It was so bad that theater goers in some South American countries threw fire bombs at the screen. Here, the audience sat mute.

But it got worse.

Before the intermission, I went outside to smoke nervously and pace the parking lot, at which point I heard a helicopter and saw that a huge space had been cordoned off in the parking lot for it to land. What the hell? A blizzard of dust and leaves and paper blew up around me and when it cleared, out of the helicopter stepped — ROGER CORMAN? Jesus, he was the director of such horror movies as the "Beast With a Million Eyes" and "The Little House of Horrors". Next stepped out the biggest-boobed woman I had ever seen, dressed in a flowing gown and walking in tight little steps on tipply spike heels. At the intermission, an announcer told everyone to stay seated for a special treat and introduced Roger with his latest star. She toddled down the center aisle to stage center, trying to counter-balance her exaggerated chest as she climbed the steps, and spoke breathlessly into the microphone: "Oh...thank you, my fans, my people...I love you all...thank you, thank you."

Row upon row of brown, unblinking faces stared silently. Some didn't understand English and none understood what was going on. Me, either. Then, she and Roger dramatically left in the helicopter.

All these memories zoomed in my head as Pancho waited for an answer.

"Si, Pancho, I know about Che."

That evening, he called us journalists together for a last group meeting and asked what we thought of them and their cause.

Francisco, the dedicated socialist, pledged his deep solidarity and passionately urged them to victory.

Ambrose wished them well and said he hoped to see them some day marching through Guatemala City with victory flags flying.

I sang "Yankee Doodle Dandy".

But first I spoke of how deeply impressed I was by what I had seen and who they were —brave fighters for a country they hoped to recreate into something good for all people. Then I struggled to convey, in my poor Spanish, how I loved my country, despite terrible things it does, because I know its heart, expressed in the Declaration of Independence with the same words Ana had used: *We are all created equal.*

As they weakly applauded, visions of James Cagney came to mind, tapping and singing the song I had always wanted to perform and now, as my toes bounced on the mud stage, was my chance. My heart swelled, my arms — elbows out — swung across my chest to the beat I tapped out with my feet, as words sung out:

"I'm a Yankee Doodle Dandy, Yankee Doodle do or die..."

Do I see grins?

"A real live cousin of my Uncle Sam, Born on the Fourth of July..."

Do I hear rhythmic clapping?

"I've a Yankee Doodle Sweetheart, She's the apple of my eye..."

Is Ana smiling?

"Yankee Doodle came to London, Just to ride the ponies,
I am that Yankee Doodle boy!"

Big finish on that last line and applause to match from the audience. They got the message: here is a Yankee who loves his country despite its blind excesses. Pancho laughed. "Very good, Terrrry," he said, embracing me. He and I and Ana moved to the fire, me between them, at ease with each other for the first time. The fire tenderly caressed our faces and we all felt warm together. Compañeros.

It was the last time I saw Ana, her head tilted down and her eyes glowing as they looked...inward. I don't know how we said goodby or even if we did, perhaps because I was too focused on what we faced tomorrow on our way back down the mountain. Pancho had warned us: "There are dangers you didn't face coming up. Many river crossings, and passages through fincas where soldiers are stationed. You will go through villages that may have spies watching. It will be much more difficult than when you came up."

That night in the champa with Geronimo

Now it was my turn to talk. The night before, he had put on his show and I understood. I wanted him to understand mine.

"I love my country as you love yours. And I have learned much about Guatemala and its struggles from you. I understand now why you are willing to give up your family and a good life to fight so that all Guatemalans have the same chances that you do. You are not the terrorist brutes that your army and government and my government portrayed you as. I have never met people like you before. I never really understood revolution before — not the one which created my country, not the civil war that saved us all from the evil of slavery, and not your revolution. But now I get it. I think of all the Mayan people I know who bend their backs to the harsh reality of their lives, do the best they can, and often go to bed hungry hurting everywhere, and wake up that way to do it again. They are chained to impossible lives like the Africans bound to their plight in my country for hundreds of years. Only the blood of many thousands of people ended their slavery and the same is true of the Mayans.

"I also, finally, understand that my government and many of its soldiers, business people and politicians have been conspiring against the Mayan people by supporting their massacre. It crushed my heart to have seen this with my own eyes before I came to this volcano and to now understand what my eyes have seen.

"You love your country for what it can be, as I love mine for what it gives my people: freedoms and opportunities your people don't. That's why I sang Yankee Doodle Dandy — to share with your compañeros how I see my country. Now I have to go back and share with my people how I see your country. To help them understand what our government is doing to you."

As he nodded, I thought of how this bright, caring, talented, passionate man and his compañeros are like students on the barricades in Les Miserables. What a courageous soul, he is, who eloquently speaks of fighting for the people and has donated his life in the act. Is he not like my favorite character in theater, Cyrano de Bergerac? Someone who loved and fought fiercely and has given up all in this pursuit. I prayed that he might escape the fate of Cyrano, who was assassinated after all the fighting was done.

Day 6

Our leave-taking in the afternoon was full of hugs, whispers of caring and even of love, and so very sad but also relief-filled. We were headed back to the world we knew and felt safe in, even if for so many people who were born here in Guatemala it was a harsh world with little hope of getting better. We would cross back over to our dimension and they would stay in theirs. I will write their story and they will keep living it. I will drink coffee and eat pastries at Dona Luisa's and the guerrillas will dream of such things as they lay in ambush among the coffee plants...and those who tend the coffee plants will arise with the sun with their hoes for a day of chopping that ends with the sun.

As I packed my few belongings, Geronimo gave me a final hug and hoped someday we would meet again, under better circumstances. It would have to be better, no? A stream of others gathered to give embraces and fond goodbyes as we started moving out in the late afternoon with a dozen compañeros. Pancho hugged me hard and repeated what he had already said many times: "Tell the world about us, Terry." His trilling of r's in my name will never be forgotten. Did I say goodbye to Ana?

And then we were gone single file into a rainstorm, the camp instantly invisible behind us as we began the dreaded guerrilla trot down through the forest. At first, it was not so dreadful for we had lived nearly a week in its deepest, most secretive barranca and were on terms with its gritty skin and hairy brush — harsh but protective. We had even started to embrace the cold and wet and fog as allies.

Fifteen hours later, during our first break, I slumped upon muddy vegetation and began writing:

"One of the worst experiences of my life. Crossed two rivers — one a dozen times as torrential rain pounded down and as lightning snapped about us. No time to fear. We pushed onward through dense rain forest. Tunnels in the growth are just high enough to let the littler guerrillas pass, but far too low for tall gringos. I fight the slapping fronds and am garroted by crawling vines. It is slippery and roots and vines trap the feet. One foot slips as the other caught. Time and again we fall, legs and ankles twisted. It is dark and treacherous. Onward we go without stopping, but the lungs and legs beg relief. Onward. Hour after hour."

The moon rose full as we dropped into cardamom fincas with their rude fronds. We wove in and out at just below a trot, soaked and hurting, and my left knee wobbled. Twice I stepped in holes, twisting its ankle, but onward without stop or pity. Tears flowed but who could tell with all the rain. Food fantasies. Bed fantasies. A promise to go home and never venture out again. Onward, down flowing erosion runs, flying down them in the dark and falling on our backs and sides and faces. The pack so wet and heavy, as are my pants and shirt and hat and wonderful Italian boots. So much pain. Vines filled with scraping stickers, tree trunks studded with spikes that slashed and stabbed. I flew down a path and grabbed a ceiba tree to make a sharp turn, but its thorns pierced my palm and held me so that I yanked backwards. My hand ripped free and I landed on my back. "Adelante!" a guerrilla urged after picking me up and pushing me forward. Back and forth across rivers in flood. A wet, mossy, muddy log stretched before me over a torrent. No! Logs that cross water are my enemy. I always fall.

"Not this time, you hoary bastard," I swore before taking my first, defiant, conquering! step.

But the enemy was in my doubting heart, not under my feet. Halfway across, I did what I knew I was going to do and only the quick, strong hand of a compañero on my backpack kept me from swirling away. Out of the river he hauled me, back onto the log onward and upward. Up, up, up. I wanted to cry, but cursed instead as my eyes filled with rain and my glasses fogged. "I can't see, I can't see," I cried, but our guides never slowed for six more hours of hell until we reached a rude camp...finally, we can stop!...but they kept going through the camp into the shadows and bush and infinity until we were forced to stop by a river so swollen it stretched wide and deep and angry and lethal, and forced us to rest. We fell upon the rocky, grassy shore, except for snake-phobic Ambrose who had heard that serpents coil in such places. He bedded down almost upright on boulders. We slept like this for two hours, so miserable, so cold.

Arriba! they told us. It was 12:30 a.m. The river was even more violent, but if we stayed the army would find and kill us. We paused at its edge, pondering the choice of river or army. One gave us a chance.

I once saw a National Geographic film that depicted ants crossing a stream by linking legs and one-by-one easing out over the water as a living bridge that quivered in the air as ant muscle struggled against gravity and breeze. It was what we did, except that we weren't above the water but in its fury, entering it one-by-one locked together with arms around each other's backs, rifles stretched across our backs... shocked and wavering and fearing we would break apart as raging water rose above my tall waist at the level of the guerrillas' chests. We were a living chain. If one link broke, we all died. Stones rolled under our feet. Unity and pride and courage from a deep place held us upright. Inch by inch. Close your eyes. Focus not on fear but on each step. Each step. Each step. Each step. Eyes open, now, to see that fear, not us, had swirled away and the river was below my belt. It had yielded and we emerged cold, shivering, alive.

No time for huzzahs and backslapping.

No stopping.

Adelante, adelante, adelante. Ni un paso atras.

Our minds turned numb. We fell automatically. We stumbled without sense. We were beaten up and yet we continued unbeaten hour after hour through cane and coffee fields, sometimes creeping along open graveled roads and feeling so vulnerable in the lights on distant hills. We snuck past sleeping compounds with armed guards, and I felt like a little boy stealing through Farmer McGregor's watermelon patch, but if we were caught it is the farmer who would be shot by rabbits. Onward into the pain. Deeper into forever. So tired we stumbled on level, smooth ground.

Finally at 3:30 a.m., we stopped in a grove of cacao trees, their canopies shaped like helmets whose sides touch the ground, creating perfect little hovels that outside eyes could not see into. Here, in these rooms, we collapsed and passed out.

Daylight woke me. I was on my back dreamily staring at a large, bulbous cacao bean hanging above me. Cacao? Ah, yes, it means chocolate, and this is a chocolate tree! Look at it up there. That delicious piece of chocolate. All I have to do is sit up, pull it to my lips, take ripping bites out of its sweet, sweet flesh. In and out of my food dream I drifted. Why must I awaken fully and know that its bitterness would make me retch?

Steam filled the tree as the warming sun rose while we lazed, licking our wounds as the guerrillas picked apart their weapons, cleaning them. Lazy, lazy day. Just one of so many boring, boring days, the guerrillas told us. It had been more than a month since their last combat — an ambush that took down many soldiers, wounded and dead. Ah well, at least there is this, they said, producing coarse unsweetened chocolate. Again I thought how ironic it was that here, where chocolate and coffee grew, we must get our pieces and sips from far away. Green parrots with yellow heads squawked in the tree top as rain and lightning and thunder returned.

Suddenly, a Mayan woman with her baby daughter in a sling across her chest came into our room, dripping. Once, she had six children, but her oldest was kidnapped by the army in March and hadn't come back. A single mother, she worked in a finca doing a man's labor in the fields of cardamom and coffee, earning $1.25 for a sunrise-sunset day. She lived far away and rose at 3 a.m. to get to work, and came home at 9 p.m. to work her shift as mother, yet she had been helping feed the guerrillas for six years despite barely having enough for her family.

"Soldiers are overbearing and arrogant," she said. "The guerrillas are ... sensible."

We spent all day and much of the night lounging, until two campesinos showed up to lead us out on the final stretch along a dirt road through small hamlets full of barking dogs. As their barks faded and the moon disappeared, a glow on the opposite horizon spoke of a new day and our guides told us the Pan American Highway was ahead. I stared into the darkness, looking for evidence, then I turned to the guides to ask where, but they had vanished. We three resumed walking in our surreaity as the new day brightened the volcanic range we had just come down and lines of streaking lights moved across our vision to the sound of...traffic! Our legs lifted faster toward civilization and safety, until we stood, amazed, at the highway edge as a bus slowed to pick us up.

The bus driver wanted money, which momentarily puzzled me. On the volcano when we tried to pay for food, they waved us off and Pancho said, "Money is nothing here." But down here in the real world, money was everything, so we dug into our pockets and bags, finally coming up with our admittance fee back into society. There was only standing room, but we were used to being on our feet, and looked into each others' eyes, and realized...

We made it.

The Escape

"The word is out — we've been discovered."

I was talking softly to Francisco and Ambrose where we huddled at a table in a corner of Dona Luisa's, drinking coffee. We looked at each other, wondering which of us had bigmouthed about our visit with the guerrillas. On the bus ride back from the volcano two weeks ago, we had vowed to stay silent lest the army find out, but ...

"Maybe it was the photographer," I said. We had dropped off our film here in Antigua with an American ex-pat who made money on the side processing and printing photos. When we went to pick them up — prints of us posing with masked gunmen — his frightened wife kicked us out with a warning to never come back. She had a family. She had a life. The war didn't exist until we brought it through her front door, which she slammed behind me.

Or maybe the army was reading our letters or had orejas who overheard us in Dona Luisa's as we talked about what we had done. Maybe we had *all* been too cocky, too mouthy.

"How do you know?" Ambrose asked.

"One of the ex-pats who lives here, a guy named Mike Shawcross, said Serrano wanted to talk with me about guerrillas."

"Serrano!" Jorge Serrano was a right-wing presidential candidate. If he knew, the army probably knew.

"I'm going to get out of here and go back to El Salvador," Ambrose said.

This was the year before the movie "Salvador" came out with actor James Wood — in his role as a freelance journalist — driving through the killing-field in his convertible, escaping one death trap after another; but that was a movie and this was real, here in Guatemala at this time when journalists were getting murdered at a faster rate than there. Ambrose's journalist friend, Nick Blake, most certainly was one.

"I'm leaving," he said and went to El Salvador. The Spaniard took off to Mexico City.

Alone. And feeling frost in my marrow like on the volcano, and running out of money.

"You have nothing to worry about," Mike Shawcross said a few days later as I sat in Dona Luisa's, my hands wrapped around a coffee cup and my eyes looking so deeply inward that it took several seconds before I realized he was sitting across from me at the little glass-topped table.

"It's Michael, by the way, not Mike," he said, correcting me good-naturedly, which is the best description of this fine fellow's attitude. He wasn't tall, but solid like a rugby player, bald and bearded, full of good cheer, and spoke like the Englishman he was, although for years now he had been one of many ex-patriates who made Antigua their home. He was still recovering from a violent motorcycle accident that nearly killed him, but he was anxious to get back to caving, his true love. Guatemala's underground was riddled with dark places to explore. Maybe I could join him, he suggested. *No shitting way.* As a kid I'd been caught by a sudden rainstorm while exploring the cave-like bowels of a drainage system in Dallas, Texas. The torrent took me, screaming with fear, through tight, dark tunnels before spitting me out.

Michael knew I was worried about talking to Serrano and said he would treat me right. He also knew about my lack of funds.

"Look," he said, "What you did has impressed a lot of people. You're not just a blowhard like so many here who jabber. You could make a life here."

A lot of people know about our venture among guerrillas? Fuck.

Michael sold antiquarian books from here worldwide, and also ran his own charity helping Mayan victims of war in the Nebaj area, my one-time Shangri-la. He wasn't rich but life was good enough, as it was for other ex-pats who did odd lines of work, like the bug man, a 40-ish, messy fellow who wore torn clothes and disappeared for weeks at time into deep jungle, capturing exotic insects for sale to universities. He got by, which was easy down here where living and life were cheap. One of the most curious ex-pats was a one-eyed chap who wore a black patch and perfectly ironed khaki safari clothes. He owned a jade mine and had a lesbian daughter who asked me over to her place so that we could experiment with her sexuality. "Maybe I am not really lesbian," she said. I never showed up and now her dad scowled at me with his good eye.

"I think you would fit right in," Michael said. As for money, well, he knew of an older single woman who was a millionaire. He would introduce me...

Fit in? Hell, I hadn't planned to make a life down here.

Fit in. Like the one-eyed man and the bug-man and Michael himself. People without a country like other ex-pats who were calling me by name and just plopped themselves down next to me at Dona Luisa's. And then, there were newcomers like Sydney.

I spotted her at a nearby table and she smiled.

Sydney was young and cute in a way that always made my legs wobble. And I was vulnerable. The girl back home hadn't written since that urgent letter I didn't answer — just before we went up the mountain. I'd been thinking more about her the last few days. She was home and country and love and safety. Sydney by contrast was a doctor who practiced healing deep in the bayous of Louisiana, where alligators and snakes and impoverished people lived; people who Sydney treated pro-bono. Helping others was her life mission, and even here on vacation she was pursuing that mission by helping the remarkable Carroll Berhorst, a world-renown doctor who had devoted his life to the poor Mayan people of Guatemala. Just the year before, he had received death threats and fled, but the echoing memories of war-orphans and sick Mayans lured him back. Sydney was intrigued when I said that I had interviewed Berhorst about the war.

"He hates how the army is massacring Mayans," I told her, "but he also thinks the guerrillas are wrong in thinking they can end the violence by using violence. He believes they should put down their arms and work with plantation owners instead of forcing them at gunpoint to improve working conditions, and shooting them if they don't. He doesn't believe you can change things all at once by armed revolution. He thinks real change comes drip by drip over a long time."

I yearned to tell Sydney that I had already shared his thoughts with the guerrillas, who thought he was naive.

"You and I could help him, don't you think?" she said.

I smiled and wanted to hug her but held back. We traded addresses and phone numbers. Please stay in touch, she said. No question. Sydney was real. Like the singer. Like Ana.

Alone again, hugging the coffee cup, I began to see new life doors opening if I was willing to radically alter the trajectory of my life. The next day, as I sat in my usual spot at Dona Luisa's typing, a fellow dressed in safari fatigues came through the door straight to my table and sat down across from me where Ambrose used to sit.

"I am Barry Sadler. Maybe you heard of me. I wrote the Green Beret song."

Of course I had heard of it. It was a hit song at the height of the Vietnam War. It was catchy, memorable. I could sing it and did—

> *Fighting soldiers from the sky*
> *Fearless men who jump and die*
> *Men who mean just what they say*
> *The brave men of the Green Beret...*

We laughed when I finished, and he started talking — boasting, actually, of having just been with the Contras, a

U.S.-sponsored group of mercenaries trying to overthrow the revolutionary Sandinista government in Nicaragua. Reagan was in deep political trouble because his administration defied Congress by secretly funding the Contras through arm sales to Iran.

"We waded across the river from Honduras with our guns held high," he said in a conspiratorial voice while leaning across the table. "Can't have the fucking commies take over down there like they did in Vietnam and are trying to do here."

I nodded, but my gut puked with disgust at his Reaganesque ignorance.

"So what are you doing down here?"

My story would blow his out of the water, and the way I'd tell it would probably make his eyes bulge with rage. But, I dared not say those words.

"Studying Spanish."

"Good for you," he said, instantly bored, and left. He was shot in the head four years later in Guatemala City. Michael showed up after he left and let me know that the Serrano interview was on for tomorrow.

"Don't worry. We are on good terms with Serrano and the government. You'll be fine."

Michael and I had argued whether former President Rios Montt got a bad rap about massacring villagers in the highlands of Nebaj. Michael spoke for a lot of ex-pats when he insisted Montt didn't know the massacres were going on, but I had a hunch that, being foreign residents, they were intuitively staying neutral and going with the political flow. I challenged him with logic.

"He was the general of the army, the president of the nation! How could he not know about the razing of 400 villages and the slaughter of tens of thousands of Mayans?"

It's complicated, he said. The previous president overreacted to the guerrilla threat and crushed it by crushing the people. Montt inherited the scorched earth policy he didn't know about. I so wanted to believe this good fellow, but his argument lacked facts.

The next day's interview with Serrano was genial until he asked how many guerrillas I thought were in the mountains. I had promised Pancho not to reveal actual numbers, so I casually said there might be 5,000.

Serrano snorted.

"Ridiculous."

He ordered his car to take me back. But I had one last thing to say.

"Comandante Pancho asked that I deliver a message — a warning — about the owner of Moca Grande finca. He's torturing his workers and not feeding them or paying them properly. If he doesn't correct his ways, the guerrillas will kill him."

Serrano laughed. Har, har.

"So, you're a messenger boy for guerrillas?"

Back in Antigua, my heart racing, I realized how badly the interview ended, but I had other things to focus on, such as a press conference in Guatemala City called by Grupo Apoyo Mutuo, made up mostly of mothers of family members who had been 'disappeared.' The woman who sang the 'Song of Guatemala' in the cornfields had said she was planning to join GAM, but though I didn't see her face in the crowd I saw her sorrow in every hard, brown face, and was awed at their courage for publicly charging the government with kidnapping and killing those who they most loved. What more did they have to lose? Their own lives? Pah! They wanted a spotlight shown upon the dark practices of a ruling class run amok. Tell the world, they told the few journalists in attendance. And find our loved ones.

My temperature dropped a few degrees, outside, when I saw that the GAM women and I were being photographed by guys in a white van with tinted windows, the favored vehicle of Guatemala's G2, their version of the CIA. They wore sunglasses and white shirts. I smiled into their lenses and heard the shutters click.

The Traitor

On the way back to Dona Luisa's, a dark memory stirred. Just before looking for guerrillas, I had attended a speech in Guatemala City given by Arnaud de Borchgrave, the internationally known editor of the Washington Times. Hundreds of well-dressed, wealthy ruling-class men filled the hall, sitting on folding chairs. I sat at the back, observing with a few other members of the press. Within minutes, I realized — to my horror — that de Borchgrave was a traitor to his profession, as he spat out lies about how the U.S. news media had been corrupted and taken over by world communism.

"There is a new school of journalism in our country, a liberal news media accountable to no one that gives more credence to radicals and communists than western governments. Right here in Central America, they report propaganda and disinformation that has undercut national security."

Heads in the room turned to look at us. Me.

"A defeat in Guatemala and Nicaragua and El Salvador will give the Soviet Union just what it wants."

Their eyes glittered and stared.

"The U.S. news media lost the war in Viet Nam and if we let them, they will lose the war down here. Don't let it happen!"

The room seethed. Suspicions confirmed! Every eye was locked and loaded and aimed at me. That day, a local journalist was killed on the street, and I blamed the savage ignorance of de Borchgrave who, like Reagan, never looked deeper than his fantasies.

The memory haunted me as I drove back to my room in Antigua, imagining that every person I passed was looking at me with suspicion. It was hard to sleep that night for I had no support down here unless I disappeared into the ex-pat community and saw no evil. I was a freelancer like the character James Wood played with no editor to call on to bail me out and running out of money. I doubted my own country would support me because it already had so much innocent blood on its hands from investing in anti-communism. I thought of the girl I left behind who was everything this place was not. She was real.

I pulled out a piece of paper. Grabbed the pen I had used to take notes on the volcano.

"Dearest..."

A gentle knock on the door startled me.

"Te busco, Terry," the young maid said. Someone was looking for me.

Oh, shit. I gritted my jaw and walked to the house's front door.

"Hi, are you Terry - the journalist?" It's a tight-faced American in his mid-20's with his unsmiling wife. We went to my room and closed the door, where they revealed themselves as anti-war activists down here to witness atrocities.

"I want you to tell my story," he said, about what happened a few days ago in El Salvador, when he was picked up by the secret police and taken to an Army airport by government soldiers who loaded him into a U.S.-supplied Huey helicopter. "U.S. military advisors watched the whole thing and did nothing as the helicopter took off and flew over the ocean. They tied my hands with rope and dangled me out the door, screaming that they were going to kill me. 'This is what we do to commies,' they said. I thought I would die."

They pulled him in and flew back to where the U.S. advisors still were, warning him that next time he'd have to swim back. "Get out of El Salvador and take all your commie shit friends with you."

"You have to tell my story," he said.

I promised to try, but was distracted the next day.

———————

A dark speck was dropping out of the sky to the west. It grew larger as it leveled off at the height of the university's tallest building — about 50 feet — and sped toward us. The students nearest me, who had been marching and raising fists and shouting slogans, paused to look up.

"Run!" a student screamed as the whop-whop of helicopter blades reached our ears and started rustling our hair.

This was the first time the army invaded San Carlos University in force since 1971 when 12,000 young people had protested the slaughter of students by President Osorio Arana, whose name everyone deliberately mispronounced as 'araña' - spider.

Today's students, who had been protesting the government's hike in bus fares, and therefore were seen as communists, started running. I stumbled along with them, looking back over my shoulder at a Huey helicopter contributed by my country to help Guatemala fight communism, and remembering a famous scene in "Apocalypse Now" when a fleet of Hueys flew just above wave tops toward a Viet Cong village. Giant loudspeakers on the helicopters blasted "The Ride of the Valkyries" as machine-gunners blasted them with bullets. I was running on the verge of panic, expecting bullets to shred my back, but what I felt was air chopped by rotor blades, blowing discarded protest signs about like roofs in a tornado. My long hair flailed. The fucking thing was overhead, and I looked up to see helmeted figures in dark uniforms panning the barrel across us like they were mowing tall grass. But they weren't shooting.

They were laughing.

Laughing at how they made the 'commie' kids shit their pants. And me, too. For one of the few times as a journalist, I felt visible and vulnerable and kept running until we were on city streets in a gauntlet of riot police swinging batons, shooting smoke grenades, and tossing tear gas canisters. Soldiers rode down the street in the back of big-tired trucks painted in camouflage, herding us toward an ending that couldn't be good. Eyes burning from my first taste of tear gas, I barely distinguished a hamburger joint off to the left and just made it inside before soldiers leaped from the truck, rifles at ready. The glass door was locked behind me, but gas still leaked under it, making my eyes weep as I watched the beat-down while sipping a Coke for about 15 minutes before I could sneak out to safety.

Back on campus, tanks were clanking and 1,500 troops prepared to invade classrooms.

At Doña Luisa's a day or so later, Michael had great news for me about a TV crew from New York in town to do a special report on Nick Blake, Ambrose's lost friend. They heard I had been searching for him and wanted me to lead an expedition into the highlands to find him.

Fucking hell no I won't, remembering the mine field and machine gun emplacements of ORPA, and knowing that Nick had disappeared into a forest of guerrillas no doubt more trigger-happy than the "sensible" ones of my experience; but I was gentle in how I turned them down, describing a jungly world of fear and hate and shoot anything that moves.

"Please." It was Nick's brother, pleading, the one who had convinced the crew to come. Wow. What a great guy. I hoped that if I ever had a lost brother that I would do no less. Nonetheless...

"No. He went in without an invitation to a wild area where not even the army is willing to go. I just came back from being with guerrillas — at their invitation — and saw how dangerous it would be without permission."

I felt terrible as I turned my back on them, feeling even more anxious than before. If a TV crew from New York knows about my trek up the volcano...

That night another soft knock on my room door, and once more it was the Maya servant.

"Te busco, Terry," she said, and I went to the front door

A dark-skinned guy in western clothing stood there with a dark look.

"Leave. They are coming for you."

"They?"

"You know." He turned and trotted off in the darkness.

Panic.

I grabbed everything I had, stuffed it in my pack and counted my money — exactly $75. Not enough for a plane ticket. The bus doesn't leave until tomorrow. What the fuck am I going to do? I walked out upon the cobbles of Antigua to Central Park and paced around. Thinking....thinking. Car headlights spotlighted me. Every passing face seemed to be looking at me. Every glittering, dark eye looked like the ones at de Borchgrave's speech. Even those of patojos. What to do? There's an American-looking guy. All touristy with his Bermuda shorts and camera around his neck. About my age. Eating an ice cream. Hey, where you from, bud? Texas? Hey, I used to live there. Dallas. Houston? Yeah, I lived there, too. Great place. Been here long? When ya leaving?

What?

He's leaving in another hour to go back to the United States. Driving his own truck.

Sure, he'll take me. He can use the company. We can share expenses.

There is a God.

His name is Steve.

He'll drop by my place on the way out of town.

I ran down the cobbled street, double-checked my gear, went outside to the curb and sat down. They have very high curbs here made of stone that channel rivers of water down the streets during heavy rain, gurgling with tiny rapids as it flows over the cobbles. It was a comfortable seat except for the murderous looks.

The truck pulled up, I threw my stuff in the back just like we did on the way to meet Ana and Pancho, and hopped in the passenger side. Steve doesn't know I am fleeing. What's the hurry? is his expression.

"I miss my girlfriend. It's been months. She's waiting for me, ya know?"

"Wish I had a girlfriend. Yassir. Sure do. Can't wait to get to Mexico."

"What's in Mexico?"

"Girlfriends."

I laughed, but was quivering. What if they had my name on a watch list at the border? I had all night to worry as we twisted and turned across Guatemala's mountainous highlands and learned about each other. Steve was a commuter airline pilot who took time off to vacation in places he usually flew over. Why Guatemala? Dunno. Drove to Mexico and just kept going. I spared him details about my predicament and told him about the bluegrass singer I was going back to see. He asked lots of questions about her. Black hair, I said. Pretty, especially when she wore long country dresses. Sang like an angel. Sounds like an angel, he said, you must love her. I'd never leave a girl like that. Why did you? I don't know. I thought I knew then, but....I'm going back now. Going home.

Steve kept asking how much longer I thought it was to Mexico. He was acting like a kid in the backseat of his parents' car. Are we there yet? I hadn't been exposed to such inane blather for months, but it kept my mind mostly off the big what-if coming up at the border a couple of hours before dawn. And the what-if kept me from shrieking out loud at Steve's crazy driving on a road I had hitchhiked home on 12 years before and memorialized with song lyrics... *a slithery mountainous way.* I wrote the words in daytime when I could see the freaky, twisting snake-back we were on, the sheer drop-offs where dead chicken buses lay crushed and rusted far below, the deep potholes that always made us yell "Whoa" or "Shit" when the truck took a dive and a slamming leap up, the little boulders we barely avoided as he drove faster than his headlights. Hours of this later, the road leveled and a blaze of light up ahead said the time for real worry was at hand. It was the border with México.

The guard at the white-painted tree trunk that dropped down before us like a train crossing arm grunted at Steve's passport and handed it back. He looked at mine and ordered, "Get out, please, and go inside."

Christ. It's come to this. After all the close calls and months of crazy.

Two soldiers with machine guns slung across their chests lounged around the doorway of the brick customs house as I entered and watched my papers being scrutinized by a highly officious man in civilian clothes. He compared my passport to a list of names on his desk and got up.

"You've been in country for a long time, Señor Winckler. What were you doing here?"

"Journalist....you know, a travel writer. Writing about what a friendly country you have. So peaceful. Not at all like what the news says. Real nice here."

"Si, señor. Please write a nice article. We need more nice tourists like you."

He stamped my passport and handed it back.

"Adios, amigo."

Steve drove us across the river and past the big painted sign: "Bienvenidos A Mexico"

"Jesus Christ," he said.

I'd just let out a spitty breath of relief on the windshield.

Girlfriends

Steve's a man in a hurry, driving fast at night. A dumb thing to do in Mexico where horses and cows idly cross roads that aren't lighted. In Tapachula itself, he slowed down, his head swiveling like he was trying to land a plane. It gave me time to look around myself and start recognizing the route I took by thumb 12 years ago when I hitchhiked back to the United States. Then, I crossed the border with seven dollars — a tenth of what I carry now, but I was happier.

Suddenly he pulled into a brightly lit parking lot in front of a building that wasn't a gas station.

"What's this?"

"Girlfriends," he said with a grin.

A brothel.

"Won't be long," he said, jumping out and running through the front door with its red-lit heart-shaped doors. He ran funny like a fella with a bursting bladder.

I laughed like I hadn't in forever as a steady stream of cars and trucks pulled up, disgorging guys dressed like cowboys with hats and boots, usually drunk and howling. Some kind of rough guitar marachi-type band music belched out each time the door re-opened, disgorging guys zipping up and no longer howling.

And then came Steve. Strolling. At ease. Nodding his head as he got back in.

He smiled at me.

"Bueno."

And we took off.

About an hour later where the lights of a small town started appearing, he slowed down again, his head twisting around. And once again we pulled into a parking lot of a building lit with red.

"Be back in 30."

And he was.

Bueno.

It was a couple of hours before we slowed down at the next town, and this time I went in with him — just to see if a brothel in Mexico looks like that one in Nebaj. Two women in satiny slips greeted Steve at the door. He chose one and disappeared through the dim inner bowels of the place with a promise to be back in 30. The other woman grabbed my arm.

"No gracias."

"Si, mi querido, don't be shy."

"No dinero."

She dropped my arm and went back to the front door as I sat down at a round table with three women already there. They were smoking. The ashtrays were heaped with wrinkled cigarette butts crusted with red crayony lipstick. They leered at me.

"No gracias."

"Si..." a hand reached across with fingers that slid across my knuckles.

"I am a maricon." Homosexual.

She patted my hand as all three tittered.

"That's ok, querido, we won't bite."

Now we could talk like friends at a local bar.

They loved the way my name sounded on their tongues with all those rrrr's and took turns trilling it. Each of them was named Juanita. We all laughed at the silly lie and started trading tales about our lives. One was a mom with three kids and three different dads who god-knows-where they are. She shrugged. It's a living. Another was 16, new to the trade and sad in her eyes. She kept her story secret. I couldn't figure out how old was Juanita Number 3. Maybe 60 by the droop of her skin all over, but she knew how to cake on makeup to fill the barrancas and fool a drunken cowboy this late at night. When she left, Steve was back. Bueno.

And so it went all the way to Mazatlan, 1,200 miles up on the western coast, mostly following the same route I had hitchhiked when only a bare trickle of migrants were with me, and now a torrent, and soon caravans from throughout Central America. As for me, the closer we got to the border, the more I thought about a bluegrass singer in a calico dress. Home.

We passed through the border at Tijuana as fast as U.S. customs would let us. They pawed through every item in the truck and asked me over and over what I had been doing south of the border. Travel writer, I kept telling them.

Finally on the other side of the border, I let out another sigh — not so much of relief as of sadness. The greatest adventure of my life was over, I told Steve. Our money's gone , too, he replied. Thieves had taken all but enough gas money to make it to LA.

"No problem. That's where my mother lives. She'll pay you for all expenses."

Mom

Mom, who had a syndicated national TV program, lived at the top of the Burbank Hilton Hotel from where you could almost see Bob Hope's walled compound. Her face exploded when she opened the door. Her eyes bulged. Her jaw dropped. Her wig shifted on her head. She screamed.

She slapped me.

"YOU SON OF A BITCH! WE THOUGHT YOU WERE DEAD!!"

She fell against me, arms clutching my neck, gasping and sobbing and shaking. Her wig fell off, revealing short gray hair full of bobby pins.

"Oh, Terry," she cried. "Why didn't you call us?"

We had left Antigua nearly three weeks before in the middle of the night without telling anyone, and Shawcross, who feared I had been "disappeared" by the Army, started looking for me. Ambrose, remembering his lost friend, Nick, headed to the U.S. to see if I was with mom, raising alarm in both of them. He returned to Guatemala to the embassy, which — led by Shawcross — looked for me in various parts of Guatemala, until they discovered I had checked out at the border. But that took some days and by then everyone was frantic as Ambrose told them reasons they should be. They also had received a roll of film I had secretively mailed that showed me encircled by guerrillas.

When mom finally stopped crying, she told me Ambrose had gone back to Central America, and she had some bad news. All the stories I had written and secretively gotten to her for sending to various publications, had been rejected. Time. Newsweek. The LA Times. San Francisco Chronicle. The Examiner.

"I don't think they believed you, son. Their own reporters down there probably told them the guerrilla threat in Guatemala had been crushed. Who were you, an unknown, to tell them different?"

All that work. All that danger. I had poured myself into getting those stories, spent hour after hour after hour writing and editing and crying over. Ana. Pancho. Don Paco. Juan Botón. Geronimo. Their names and faces and the heartbeats they trusted me with played across my thoughts like the streaming headlines on a TV newscast. All for naught. "Tell the world," they begged. I had failed.

"Suzanne called."

My heart flipped.

"About a month ago. She hadn't heard from you. Just checking in. Told me to say hello."

She was only a two-hour drive away.

I picked up the phone.

And this time I dialed.

"Suzanne?"

"Oh, Terry."

I told her I would be there soon. I'd meet her at her parents' house. I thanked Steve for everything and found a picture of Suzanne to show him.

"You're a lucky, guy," he said.

———————

It was like driving through Guatemala, again, not knowing what to expect at the border. But I was in my good, ol' 1965 Olds Cutlass convertible again — a lot like the one James Wood drove in the movie "Salvador." It had never failed me.

It was nearly dark when I pulled up in front of her parents' house. The light was on and she heard me drive up. The door opened. I saw her dark hair. She wore a long dress with straight sleeves that shivered as she ran down the porch steps and onto the driveway too fast for me to get out before she opened the passenger door and slid in.

"Oh, Terry," she cried, and we fell into each others arms, trembling as we hugged long and hard. Shaking and crying into each others' ears. She turned her face to me, but as I went to kiss her lips, she pulled back and sat stiff with her hands in her lap, looking forward, saying nothing for a long time as I breathed hard.

"Oh, Terry." She looked at me with steady, drying eyes, and her voice was calm. "You should have called."

There was another she was going to marry.

Time Runs Out

Tito entered the long, dark night

A Slow Death

As I mourned a lost love and went on with my life, Guatemala's revolutionaries struggled to keep their cause from being lost in a limbo of not-winning-not-losing.

ORPA and its three allied groups still ruled the remote tip-tops and canyons of Guatemala, but in the corridors of power — in the cities and especially in THE city — they were seen as a handful of fleas the big dog scratched from time to time. They were irrelevant, Serrano, the future president, had told me with a snort of contempt. But they weren't defeated. The sensible leadership of ORPA stayed true to Che's playbook by avoiding suicidal head-to-head combat in the flats where the army could easily mobilize its vastly superior forces. Che's first rule was to stay alive to fight another day.

Another day, another day, another day...

The days turned into weeks and months and years of survival — a grueling time for those whose faith in the cause kept them warm. They had pounded their feet on the mud for me, singing "Libertad! Libertad! Libertad!" but years passed and faith corroded. The pounding of feet became less about the cause and more about fighting their most relentless enemies - the wet, the cold, the irrelevance.

———————

One morning in 1988, Capitan Julio woke as usual, put on his clothing and, around 6 a.m., walked down the mountain to become Tito again.

He wasn't the first to quit the revolution. Long before he breathed his last for ORPA, its fighters had been leaking off the volcano, but Tito's departure was more ominous than most. He had been with them eight years as one of the truest of true believers, the poetic kind who had absorbed the cause until it flowed within him like blood itself — the hot blood that made him brave in the early years when soldiers came up the volcano brutish as burros, seeking a foe that looked like trees in the forest. They blindly followed paths straight up the volcano, rather than slithering about in the secretive, snakelike way of guerrillas taking advantage of terrain. They marched into deep canyons as the guerrillas strategically moved to high ridges and pounded the soldiers below, forcing them to flee down into an ambush of mortars, machine guns, mines, and rockets. Tito grinned in appreciation of one such attack.

"We were resting in an open place of thin trees when I saw a soldier suddenly rise up some distance away. I shot him with a spray of bullets and then we all lay still in the grass as the rest of them came toward us. We didn't see them, but when we saw the bushes shake, we shot until the bushes stopped moving, then we fled upwards to the top edges and laughed as army aircraft pounded where we had been with bombs."

But the army was learning. It, too, became the wily snake and sometimes ambushed guerrilla camps, killing instead of being killed. ORPA found itself on the move, volcano to volcano, still masters of terrain but forced to cover more of it to stay alive. Its fighters fought peek-a-boo style within the volcano chain that stretched from Pacaya at the edge of Guatemala City to the greatest of them all — Tajamulco — highest point in Central America, near the Mexican border. But, peek-a-boo is a game. Is that why they became guerrillas? It was supposed to be a tactic not the reason to be there. Yet, Tito, like most, kept the faith, and even though they were isolated from the big picture of a revolution crushed in most of the country, he believed in the big picture of hope painted by Ana and Pancho and Santiago and ORPA's founder, Gaspar Ilom.

Then something happened that shook Tito's faith in the leadership and ultimately in the cause. He won't say what it was, only that it opened his ears to his mother's warning eight years before when she begged him not to go up the mountain: "They will lie to you." It turned him against Pancho and Gaspar, who Tito thought of as a kind of coffee shop leader. It may be an unfair view, but it is Tito's and of others who lived on the bitter spear point while Gaspar stayed in the comforts of Mexico. Perhaps they didn't know that Gaspar's sick feet were no longer capable of walking in a guerrilla's boots.

The leaders were good at fighting battles on volcanoes, Tito thought, but they could never win the war, and what if they did? They couldn't lead a country. He never stopped loving or trusting Ana and admired her open distaste of Gaspar's directives, but she was a priest not a pope.

Tito began shaking with a fear he couldn't shake.

———————

As he talked in 2019, it was as if he was back on the volcano, watching Ana by the river. His voice was the willow tree whose thin branch drooped to the surface of slow moving water, tracing a line of thoughts that stopped and started as the branch dipped in and out of his depths. "I asked myself: why do you want to be a hero? All I want to do is help people." He paused as the branch lifted its quill before dipping back in. "For the first time, I became afraid of dying for no reason."

He began seeing the death of friends and enemies as empty acts, and the weight of it dragged him into bleakness illuminated by a single spark: the guerrillera who cleansed wounds. One poor fighter had lost all the flesh on part of his body, but this tender woman cleaned the exposed bone so gently. "Wow," Tito thought, "All the guys loved her because of what she did. She was not a nurse or doctor, just an idealistic woman, a beautiful woman helping. Wow."

But why were there wounds to begin with? What was the point? The leaders were in it for themselves, for THEIR cause not THE cause, he started thinking. Doubt ate his faith. Eight years Tito had lived on the mountain and he saw no end of living there, he told Pancho.

Pancho ordered him to leave.

———————

It took nearly two days, along the same route I had taken with my journalist pals, for Tito to reach the Pan American Highway, walking off all the fear and pain and doubt and suffering, just as we had. And, as he got into a waiting car, he experienced the same gushing sensation of relief we felt on the bus. "My God, at last I am free. Wow, there is no fear and I feel like the wind and like a new man. I am so happy. So happy to leave the fight."

On the way to Mexico, he ate shrimp. That night he slept in a real bed.

"I felt normal again after so many years of seeing my friends die. After all the experiences. I had lived 10 lives in those eight years....a long, long journey to another galaxy."

But no one is normal like they used to be after going up the mountain.

Tito entered the long, dark night of the soul that many ex-warriors experience when their heads rest on soft pillows in safe places.

"I was dead, really dead. I didn't know who I was when I went down the volcano. No dreams, no ideals, only nightmares and sadness and wondering 'Who am I?' as I stayed within my room for a year. This is the price I had to pay for what I did.

"And I am not glad I did it."

Josue "Geronimo", on the other hand, loved his 14 years on the mountain.

"It was a marvelous experience," he said in 2019, even though his wife and two children had abandoned him after years of not hearing from him, something he will never get over. Ironically, it was his wife's idea for him to go up the mountain, to avoid being killed by death squads. Being a city boy, though, that first three-day hike upwards with a fifty-pound pack almost killed him. His body rebelled in the strangest way.

"I farted constantly."

Farting, huffing and puffing, Josue was the only one to reach camp out of 15 who started. The rest dropped out for various reasons. There, he took on the war name of the great Apache chief and was quickly thrown into battle. It was 3 a.m. as they dug in for an ambush against the army.

The enemy suddenly swarmed him. A swarm of ants. Geronimo had dug into a nest of them and retreated outside the hole, preferring to fight soldiers. He fled back to the hole when firing broke out and discovered the creatures had disappeared. So, too, had the birds though their voices shrieked. Thus it was during every battle. It's a lesson he applied later when, as chief mine maker, he set mine-traps. When the birds suddenly start screeching, "Boom!"

Forty soldiers died in this first of many combats he fought, and he wept over those killings in 1985 each night as we talked. "I hate it, I hate it, I hate it!" Hated it enough that all these decades later he regrets doing it?

"Hell, no!"

The volcano chain that ORPA ruled over was Josue's grand stage. From peak to peak, in their deepest bowels, amid storms and wet and battles and star-filled nights, he lived out stories that would have inspired Shakespeare. And finally, on Volcano Tajamulco — highest point in Central America — he was able to put down his gun and pick up his greatest weapon: a microphone. From those heights, using a clandestine radio, he poured out news of the revolution across a swath of Guatemala. It was glorious, he said. The experience transformed him. Changed his life. Gave him spine. Made him a good person.

"Otherwise, I would have been a drunk."

On the mountain, one night in the tent we shared, he had whispered of his dream to be in theater when it was all over. And that's what happened when he went down the mountain. He became director of Guatemala's National Theater and then a teacher at the same university where he learned to be a revolutionary. We met there in 2019 during a student strike he was shepherding. I hadn't been at the university since the student strike of 1985 when the army descended on us with tanks and a helicopter. On this day, without a uniform in sight, the students gathered in the rotunda of an elegant building and declared victory. One of them, a bright-faced smart fellow almost as tall as me, was helping translate. Our conversation seemed to stun him, especially when Josue talked of being a celibate for 14 years as a revolutionary.

"No woman wanted me."

"Your tactics are too soft. These are warrior women up here that need to be conquered," a compañero said, laying out a six-point plan for how to do it — a rapey kind of plan that

Josue had no stomach for. Just like the girl I left behind, he thought about the wife he left behind, and after the war traced her to the United States, but she had re-married and wanted nothing to do with him, nor did his three children who accused him of abandoning them. Which of course he had. Though he has since found love with another woman, the pain of his lost family is forever in him. Like Tito, he paid a grievous price.

And like Tito, he had been mesmerized by Ana - "a great human being. Happy, cheery, confident and brave. She loved to fight!"

"And beautiful, no?"

"Especially, her ideas. She taught about why we were there — to bring equality to the Mayan people."

I wanted to cry when he spoke the exact words I had written down as he talked to me in the night 34 years before: "To know why you are fighting — for something greater than you — is what makes you brave and willing to die."

––––––––––––

The student translator is having a hard time keeping up. He struggles to convey Josue's spillover of thoughts and information, and he struggles to believe what he is hearing. His teacher, this humorous and dramatic old fellow who stood before him, had been a guerrilla captain? Had made mines from tree sap and led ambushes in the neblina? The student seemed completely ignorant of the civil war that had consumed his country for 36 years, ending before he was even born; that his university had been a breeding ground for the revolution, and that the war itself had been such an enormous event. Like every young person I spoke to over two years, he knew little about it. It hadn't been taught except as something of a throwaway line in school. An event that shook this country to its foundation hardly existed for his generation. Even Josue had barely mentioned it to his students.

"They made funny quizzical faces when I brought it up."

When he used the word "genocide" in the context of headlines about a truth commission, one of his students said she would talk to her father about it — an army colonel. There was no genocide, he told her. Fake news. As if 200,000 mostly Mayan deaths hadn't happened.

As Josue talks, the young translator stares with open-faced admiration. With amazement. To think that such things were stirred here on his campus, by his professor, by students like...him.

"I don't know why Josue was happy," Tito says. "Maybe his story is different than mine. I saw my compañeros killed by the army. And for what reason? It is very, very sad for me. That's why I tried to run away from talking about it because it takes me back to the suffering, to the death of many, many young people."

He got through it - with the aid of that young, beautiful woman on the volcano who cleansed his heart as she did the grievous wounds of their compadres. They had two children together.

But they split up.

Saber — who knows why?

Hernan also stayed to the end and is at peace with himself. When he talks of those times, I see the smiling guerrilla sitting in a photo in front of Ana. He is upbeat, despite some ailments, most notably the missing finger on his right hand, lost when a weapon blew up during the last great guerrilla action of the war. He also lost two brothers to the war, including one whose body wasn't discovered until 2017, yet, like Josue, he stayed a true believer in ORPA to the end and today lives with his family in one of the most curious places in Guatemala. It's called Colonia Diciembre 29 — December 29, the date peace accords were signed in 1996, officially ending the "conflict" as the war is euphemistically called these days. The colonia was established as part of the accords to provide housing for ex-guerrilleros like Hernan. It is hidden well-off the main highway, reachable only by a dirt road that ends at a monument topped by a statue of a guerrilla holding a weapon at the ready. The town itself is rife with crime, but not the colonia. Who would dare?

Eventually, Tito pulled himself together, came back to Guatemala and started a design studio. Alone, he lives what he calls his "second life" in a peaceful, upscale neighborhood of Guatemala City, behind walls. Often, he walks to a nearby park full of trees and twittering birds and playing children. It sits on the edge of a deep forested canyon not unlike those he once lived in as a guerrilla. I breathe in a melody of natural fragrances as he sits on a park bench, staring into the depths of the canyon.

"Before it became a park full of children, Terry, this is where the death squads dumped tortured bodies."

Vultures float on its updrafts.

In the years after Tito left, others also lost hope and left, among them some of the most senior members. All of the four guerrilla factions that made up the united front suffered defections as the era of Central America revolution faded. Nicaragua's revolution had ended in 1979 with a triumphant march, but its war leaders struggled to lead it in peace against increasing anti-communist efforts by the U.S. Cuba, the spawning ground for revolution, still provided training and its fiery leader kept giving pro-revolution speeches and encouragement, but, as time passed, Castro's words were hardly better than thoughts and prayers for revolutionaries in Guatemala.

By 1992, ORPA and its allied groups were fighting the last revolution in Central America. It was the year El Salvador's bloody civil war ended with a peace treaty. The year that the Mayan woman Rigoberta Menchu won the Nobel Peace Prize. Desperate by year's end, some guerrillas threw out Che's playbook and took a dramatic act of self-rescue. In direct contradiction of the mandate to avoid head-to-head battle with the army on its grounds, guerrillas flooded off the volcanoes and mountains for one last push. ORPA, in Pancho's absence, commandeered the mighty volcano Agua looming over Antigua.

The unified forces struck at the edges of urban areas throughout the heart of Guatemala, sending a shock wave through the media and government. The army, which had been tipped off, quickly retaliated, killing guerrillas wholesale as it crushed the attacks. Pancho, who was in Mexico, bitterly wrote of the poor tactics and of a comedic-tragic incident. His former fighters were huddled in a cornfield above Antigua, so hungry that a leader ordered dinner from a nearby Campero Chicken restaurant. Army forces followed the delivery vehicle, surrounded the guerrillas, and killed more of them than this ORPA group had sustained in any previous battle. The handful of survivors snuck back to the safety of volcano Atitlan. As a military tactic, the attack was a devastating failure, but it succeeded as a political coup. Now, not even the most stubborn guerrilla wanted this unending stalemate to continue. Serious peace talks resumed in Mexico City, where Santiago, Pancho and Ana were living.

It was the last November of Ana's life.

The Reunion

2017

"Comandante Pancho" and author reunite

The Ex-Comandante

As migrant caravans full of children flooded out of Central America toward cages at our border, my son Casey — who just graduated high school — came to me.

"Dad, I want to go alone to Central America."

Gut-punched.

"What do you think, dad?"

I can't think. But, hell no, you can't go. You're only 17.

"Dad?"

"Your mother will freak out."

"That's why I came to you - I need your help to convince her."

I need convincing, but what do I tell you — not to do what I had done, not to do what I filled your childhood with stories about? Not to have a Hemingway heart? Not to be bold and audacious and questing? But, you are so young and the world you want to go off into is so ...

"What do you think, dad?"

I think of you weeping last year when I took you fishing at a place sacred to me — Black Rock Pass. Your heart had exploded like the speckled head of the brook trout I just smashed with a rock.

'Dad, o dad,' you cried as tears made little puffs in the dust. 'He was so beautiful, so beautiful.'

"Dad?"

"Let me talk to your mom."

"Are you fucking crazy?"

Laura, herself a journalist, is stunned that I would even consider letting our 17-year-old son Casey go alone to Central America.

"The headlines are full of stories about drug cartels and murders and violent robberies in Central America, and he is just a boy."

Laura knows about such things — she was robbed twice at gunpoint of all her camera equipment in Oakland, a city connected to ours by three short bridges. *Is Central America more risky?*

"I did it when I was young and there was a war back then."

"Why do you think people are fleeing to our border nowadays?"

"Well..." She had a point. Back then, there were only two sides - revolutionaries and the governments they were trying to overthrow. Now there are many sides, and numerous people are killed every day because of drugs, gangs, corruption and poverty; and there is corrupt governance, which forced many onto marginal land that barely feeds them as climate change adds its woe of altered weather patterns. The only hope for many is the road north — the same one I hitchhiked happily home on in 1973, and fled on in 1985.

As I pondered, she spoke again...this time softly in a tone I knew so well.

"This isn't about Casey, it's about you. As long as I have known you, you have wanted to follow your heart back to Guatemala and find answers about people like Ana. This may be your only chance. Go. Take Casey with you and teach him how to travel. If you think it's safe, turn him free."

My heart stuttered. She had just opened the door to my past if I was willing to get back on that road.

So, how does one find an ex-guerrilla commander whose last address was a camp in a canyon on a volcano 3,000 miles and 32 years away?

By Facebook of course.

It took 30 seconds to find Pancho's page and 10 seconds to send a message: "Do you remember me?"

Shortly, came the reply: "Te recuerdo." I remember you.

Three weeks later, Casey and I were in Guatemala City, stopped at a barricade as armed men approached, arousing memories. *These guys guarding the way to Pancho's place in the city are different than those guys three decades ago guarding the way to Pancho's place on the volcano.*

These guys, strolling openly around the entrance to a walled-off cluster of neighborhoods, are dressed like soldiers with shiny black boots, crisp white shirts and dark berets. One holds a sawed-off shotgun with a pistol grip. The other casually touches a machine gun draped across his chest on a strap. They smile when my identification is approved and the barrier pole lifts.

"Bienvenidos," says the one with a shotgun, gesturing for us to pass.

The genial contradiction makes me smile, and I turn to Casey, sitting in the passenger seat of our rented car, staring at machine-gun man. As we drive through the guard post, his wide-open eyes turn to me.

"He seems friendly."

"That's because we are expected. And one thing I know is that you don't go looking for guerrillas - or even ex-guerrillas — without an invitation."

Casey's heard the story before - of how I came to Guatemala in 1985 as a reporter in the midst of civil war and, with two reporter pals, discovered guerrillas hiding in forests among the country's spectacular volcanoes. They weren't supposed to be there in any real numbers. The army said they had been crushed years before. But, there they were, ruling the western heights of Guatemala and anxious to let the world know that the revolution still lived. That's why they invited me and my pals to come up for a look.

"Those guys in the forest — the guerrillas who guarded the trail up the volcano — wore olive green for disguise and the first thing we saw of them were machine gun barrels sticking out of the undergrowth as we ran by. Instead of shooting, they grinned."

Casey is too busy to talk. His head swings left and right as we drive down a clean, bright concrete street. If he's looking for bearded warriors, all he sees are mothers and children strolling sidewalks past well-groomed front yards with thin trees and tropical plants drooling colors. The homes look like ours in California. Some Spanish colonial, some modern condo. All kinds. Our kind. After a few blocks, we pull up to an impassive black metal gate, at least 10 feet high and 20 feet across. Another guard with a handgun at his belt stands in an open doorway of the gate.

"Why do they have walls?"

"Because they have wealth and most Guatemalans don't. Remember that headline in today's paper about 26 Guatemalans being killed every day because of drugs and gangs linked to poverty?"

How ironic. Pancho has to wall himself off from desperate conditions he once fought to change.

The guard is finished scanning our IDs, our faces, our car, and nods his head.

"You'll find him up the road in Number 10," he says while grunting to push open the creaking gate. "He's waiting for you."

Waiting for me, just like before.

To calm myself, I take extra care as I park the car, open its door and get out to walk the last 50 yards up a slightly rising narrow street. It is a mild, sunny day with cloud puffs drifting across the sky. It was uphill the first time I sought Pancho, straight up the volcano...at night...in thick cloud forest as rain and wind and lightning and thunder pounded us — three journalists and our guerrilla guides.

Back then, I was going to meet a commander of guerrilla forces. Today, my son and I are coming to meet Pedro Pablo

Palma Lau, the name Pancho reassumed after spending 20 years — his entire youth — fighting Central America's most vicious army. Pancho is the war name he adopted to keep the Army from knowing who he really was, lest they torture friends and family members into betrayal.

No one betrayed Comandante Pancho. He survived to walk down from the volcanoes as the 36-year civil war ebbed away, and rebuilt his life under the name he had been born with. My left hand clutches tight around his memoir as Casey and I walk up the street. A man appears ahead of us.

"Pedro?"

"No."

He gestures to a small two-story house on my left. A simple condominium-style home with parking underneath. So this is where a revolutionary goes when he puts down his guns. An odd thought - do I call him Pancho or Pedro? I know one but not the other. After three decades, I wonder how well he remembers me — someone who suddenly appeared and disappeared after five days, only to pop up on Facebook three decades later. There are questions, so many mysteries to clear up about his life after I left Pancho; but there is really just one question I must have answered: What happened to Ana? His memoir lamented her death, but didn't say how or why she died, and his Facebook feed has been littered with questions about her. The most critical suggest that Pancho is withholding a dark secret.

And now I am at Pedro's door, hesitating to knock. My raised fist hovers to the beat of my heart.

Does he really remember me or was he just being polite? It's been so long. So much has happened in both our lives. So many people — generals, presidents, soldiers, judges, journalists — have filled his years.

"Go ahead, dad," my son urges.

I slam my knuckles against the heavy wooden door.

Silence.

Is he even home?

Soft rustling from inside. The door knob kind of rattles and turns. The door opens tentatively, creaking.

And there — supported by the door frame — stands a man with the strong, square face of Pancho and the tilted, swaying, broken body of an old man. He leans on a cane. His joints seem loose. He has shrunken from the six-footer I knew. His beard is gone. But his gaze into my eyes is as familiar and strong as that commander in the forest.

"Terry," he whispers, trilling the rr's of my name in a familiar way, dropping his cane, reaching out his arms, and falling into my arms, his left cheek brushing my right one as he kisses it and wets it with his tears, and breathes my name again.

Jesus Christ, what's happening? I didn't expect tears and hugs and kisses, and all this hot adrenaline flooding me with emotions.

"Te recuerdo, Pancho," I say softly into his ear, clutching him like a lover.

We pull back finally and gaze upon each other at arm's length.

"I remember you, too, Terry."

I wonder what my face looks like. His is rumpled like a baby's after a cleansing cry.

"Please, my dear friend, enter," he says, making way for my son and I to enter.

ORPA guerrillas with Pancho (standing middle) and Ana

The door softly closes behind us.

Pancho leads us through his small, artfully arranged home, sprinkled with photos of his time as a revolutionary — brave portraits from a time so far away. The largest framed photo, looking formally posed in a forest setting, shows three smiling fighters in the foreground. Ana smiles off to the left, her disheveled hair pulled back with a head band. Sitting in front of her are the guerrillas Hernan and Hector, also smiling. Pancho stands behind them, beaming like a proud papa. Santiago, a bearded grim man in fatigues, stands to his left. Only Santiago's name is not within my notebooks.

"Beautiful, Pancho! Who took it?"

"A compañero snapped it just before we thought the Army would kill us. Soldiers had surprised us and pushed us up the volcano until we could go no farther. We were almost surrounded. Do you see that canyon to the right? Behind me hidden by forest is a steep cliff. We were trapped and thought our time had come, so we decided to make a last photo. We had lived well, fought well, so why not be happy at the end?"

"But you survived."

He laughs.

"The soldiers were afraid. These were my best fighters and they knew it. They retreated."

I look slowly over the rest of his place, trying to get a feel for the life he is now living.

"A fine hand has been at work decorating," I say.

He points to a picture of an attractive woman. "Anaite." His wife has the same-sounding name of that other Ana. "I stole her from a millionaire in Mexico," he says with a wink and hobbles off on his cane to get water glasses, which he fumbles, so I go to his side and take them.

"Gracias, Terry. It is hard to walk after so many golpes (physical punishments) in the mountains." Pancho's spine is tweaked. He lost ribs to a surgeon's knife. His bowed legs and hips hurt. Sixteen years on the run. Yeah. His voice, though soft, is strong.

He pours sparkling water from a glass pitcher, reminding me of the first drink Pancho poured for me — rum — in the

The sons

rain and mud of his cloud forest home on the volcano named
Atitlan.

"Salud," he says, as we clink glasses. In the mud we toasted freedom — "Libertad!" And he toasted my good fortune at
having made it safely to a hideout encircled by soldiers. "You
are lucky," he told us. "Others were killed looking for us."

He turns to my son, who is gazing at him with almost
a stare.

"Your father is very brave — muy valiente!"
Casey glances at me with a smile.

My chest almost explodes with pride. Lives there a dad who doesn't want his son to believe such a thing? My dad was dying of old age before I stumbled upon proof of his bravery in World War II and the stories he told. I barely had time to apologize for my years of thoughtless jests before he died.

Pleasantries over, I start asking questions, but it isn't going well, as we both have mostly forgotten the other's language. All of our conversation so far has been halting and difficult with much hand wringing and pieced together bits of Spanish and English.

"I speak better English before," he says apologetically.

"Yo spoke *mejor* Spanish."

We stumble over our tongues for a few minutes until a young man enters through the front door.

"My son, Francisco."

The son is 27 and shorter than his father — even this smaller version — but there are hints of Pancho in the shape of his face, the strength of his chin, and the hair on his upper lip. Pancho thinks he favors his mother, but when I look at Anaite's face in the photograph, I don't see similarities.

"Perhaps," I say. His mustache is heavier and blacker than the one his father wears in the photograph. He has deep, dark, familiar eyes. He is reserved and polite and speaks excellent English. Through his translation, the conversation instantly takes off on an unexpected tangent.

"Francisco and I love American music, especially Chuck Berry."

"Chuck Berry, the father of rock and roll, who just died?"

"Did you like him?" he asks.

"Like him? He was our first client when my mother and I started a public relations agency, before I became a journalist."

A bomb under Pancho's chair could not have elevated him higher or quicker.

"YOU KNEW CHUCK BERRY!!?"

Pancho is dumbfounded and I am dumbfounded that he is. His eyes and face and wide-open mouth freeze in what appears to be shock, and he clutches his hands together against his chest in reverie.

"Mom and I promoted a Chuck Berry fundraiser for the U.S. Olympic volleyball team. It was wild. When he died I wrote a story about it on Facebook."

Since Pancho and I are connected on Facebook, it is easy for his son to find the story and — with great animation — translate it out loud in Spanish as his father, now oblivious to the aches and pains of his past, rocks back and forth in joy. He blasts out laughter at the part about mom telling Chuck to "get the fuck out on stage and play" when he demanded money in advance.

"I CAN'T BELIEVE YOU KNEW CHUCK BERRY!" he shouts at me in Spanish.

Francisco is smiling and laughing and showing real emotion for the first time.

Casey is transfixed.

After more excited banter, the conversation finally simmers and we turn back to our shared story. I pull a boxy old tape recorder from my satchel and place it on the table between Pancho and Francisco.

"This is a recording of an interview made in your camp on the volcano when I visited you as a journalist."

"Ahhh," says Pancho, leaning forward in his easy chair. "Is it me?" He shows the semi-grin I remember so well about him.

"No, it's Ana."

"Ana?" he says softly, losing the grin.

Pancho looks to his son seated across the living room. Francisco stares back impassively.

"Are you ready to hear this?"

Francisco nods.

I am confused.

"Why wouldn't he be ready?"

Pancho looks back at me.

"He's never heard his mother's voice."

Now, *my* face freezes. I drop my notebook to the rug and choke out a question.

"*Ana...* is his mother?"

All this time I thought his mom was Anaite.

"Ana died when he was a baby...She was murdered."

Murdered!? I knew she was dead, but... Pancho won't reveal more details despite my flurry of questions, so I turn to Francisco, staring at me with eyes that suddenly seem familiar.

"Are you ready?"

Francisco nods and Ana's eyes glow as I push the recorder's button.

It begins with the night sound of crickets — background to a calm, clear, soft, strong woman's voice that flows out in silvery Spanish with carefully rolled r's and carefully expressed thoughts.

"It is a very, very hard life being a guerrilla..."

Instantly, Pancho's face is in his hands.

"...but it is a very satisfactory life..."

Pancho is sobbing.

"Here in the mountains, we are all equals..."

Francisco's head droops. He picks tears one by one from each eye.

"Our fight is to make all Guatemalans equal..."

My face has fallen into my hands and every finger is wet.

Ana continues for a few minutes as crickets chirp and men weep.

The hard snap of the tape stopping jolts us back into the moment.

Casey is a statue as we try to compose ourselves.

Ana's voice has taken us high up a volcano into the time-altering neblina, within a deep and thickly forested canyon to a campfire where compañeros are gathering at day's end to tell stories, share adventures, mourn the fallen, praise the heroic, and to huddle close for warmth against the wet cold. We talk and huddle for hours until deep in the night when we are too exhausted to continue, drained of energy and even of tears. Pancho and I agree to meet again, and the door closes gently with a click behind Casey and I as we stumble out into a very dark night lit by very dim streetlights, but Casey is very awake and grabs me by the shoulders.

"WHAT THE FUCK JUST HAPPENED IN THERE, DAD!?!"

His outburst stuns me.

"It was like a movie!"

A movie?

I never thought of it that way before. But I do now as I stare into my son's agitated face and imagine what he just experienced, sitting as if in a theater while stories leaped around him like animated flames in the campfire. Images — scenes! — of people at each other's throats in a civil war bloodier than any other on a continent broiling with revolutions. He heard tales of patriotic love and romantic love and genocidal hate, of ambush and massacre, of winning battles but not the revolution, and — *oh, Ana* — of treachery.

"He said you were brave, that you almost died, that you were lucky to escape, that other journalists were killed doing what you did. You never told me that!"

Casey is shaking me with his hands and emotions.

"What else didn't you tell me?"

We have a crazy, wild drive ahead of us through the night madness of Guatemala City traffic, a macho-fueled, rules-free combat zone that makes it hard to concentrate as I tell him things I've been thinking about for two-thirds of my life. The story continues in the quiet of our hotel room in the ancient city of Antigua, as an old church bell rings, chiming in like an exclamation point until it and my lips fall silent, leaving Casey and I staring at each other, knowing that my story was ending and his was about to begin. The next day we traveled to Lake Atitlan where I pointed out the grand volcano where I met the guerrillas, and the next morning he shook me awake, whispering, "It's time, dad."

Soon, we are walking a narrow mud path through corn and coffee plants to the concrete road rising up to the nearby village. He is burdened with possessions on his back, as I am burdened inside, and we both walk heavily. Ahhh, I hope I am doing the right thing. I want to cry out like the poet don Paco: *Aieee! He is going away, this young son of mine. My boy. I pray that you will be safe through places people are fleeing from. I have taught you all I know about navigating wilderness, but the snakes here are different than those in the Sierra.*

Loud, angry sounds greet us on the main road, made by three-wheeled tiny taxis called tuk-tuks that dart around, powered by motorcycle engines. One stops ahead of us and its young driver waves. This is it. Casey turns to me and we hug like Pancho and I did — with cheek kisses and tears and whispers of love. Then he spins, jumps in and sticks his head out looking at me as the taxi takes off, making the sound of a boy leaving home.

Tuk

Tuk

Tuk.

He vanishes into traffic and the passage of time. *Go with God, dear son. Be safe.*

Jingling bells startle me. It's an ice cream cart pushed by the teen-aged son of another father. This kid is dressed all white in rough woven cotton pants and shirt with a blue sash belt, lots of showy, white teeth, skin the color of my favorite dark coffee and thick, black, uncombed hair like Casey's.

"Helado, señor?"

What's this sudden gushing emotional release of tension?

I feel relief and lightness, just as Casey must. At last he is free to step out of my footprints to make his own, and I am free to retrace mine. Whistling, I buy a pink, coconut-frosted ice cream on a stick and lick it like a dog. It tastes happy! I jump on my own tuk-tuk back to the hotel and call Pancho to set another meeting to discuss what really happened to Ana.

"TERRRRRY!"

Pancho is grinning as he struggles from the Uber car outside my hotel. It seems a lifetime since we last met with my son, although only two weeks have passed. Tomorrow, I will meet Casey at the airport to hear about his solo adventure through Central America, but tonight it's just Pancho and me and a lot of questions. Once again, we hug fondly. I help him up the steps and across the lobby, not just because of old war wounds but because of what he is carrying — a heavy object in a brown paper bag.

It's difficult getting down the stairs, through the hotel garage, and down another set of stairs to my room, but, though broken in body, the old comandante is bursting with spirit.

Inside the room, he puts the object down on the table with a thump.

"Do you have two glasses?"

Of course, but first this. I pull from my bag a small object in a plastic bag that I had revered for decades.

"Your pipe, Pancho."

It's the briar pipe with the black stem that had bite marks from a man who had chewed it in concentration on the volcano. He had given it to me as a parting gift. His eyes know that pipe. He accepts it reverently, turning it as the memories flicker across his face. He had taken it from the desk of a plantation owner who brutalized workers. It reminds him of why he fought all those years. He tries to hand it back, but I resist.

"Un regalo para ti — a gift for you."

"NO! It is yours. It was the gift of one friend to another. Keep it forever."

He turns to the bag on the table and reaches into it.

"Un regalo para nos mismos — a gift for us both."

It's a huge bottle of tequila. Bigger even than the bottle of Castro's rum he shared on the volcano.

"Oh, Pancho. Don't you remember? I don't drink."

"Of course you do."

"I'll drink coffee instead."

"You're drinking tequila!"

"No."

"YES!"

His face tenses as he reaches for my glass.

"No," I say, grabbing his hand. It is strong but mine is unmoveable. This isn't that other dimension on the volcano where life was lived in gulps.

We stare into each others' faces across the decades.

"My last drink was with you on the volcano. I won't have another."

His face reddens. Will he punch me?

Pancho drops into a chair with a long sigh.

"Bueno. Coffee for you."

And tequila for him. He pours a full glass.

"Salud!"

The night ignites.

We talk idly at first. He grins when I tell him about letting Casey go alone to Nicaragua.

"He is his father's son."

"And your son, Francisco?"

Pancho shakes his head slightly. Francisco is having troubles. He mourns a mother whose voice he didn't know when I played it for him.

"He has a hole in his heart."

He pours another glass.

"Tell me about how Ana died."

"She came down from the mountain to give birth to Francisco and be a mother to Alejandra."

"Alejandra?"

"Her daughter. She was, I think, 15."

"A daughter?"

This is how I first learned that, before meeting Pancho, Ana was married to the guerrilla Marco, and had a daughter with him. Pancho, now into his second glass, doesn't want to talk about any of that or about her death, so I switch subjects. Why did he come down the mountain and join the political party of the genocidal Rios Montt and twice get elected to Guatemala's Congress in alliance with him?

Pancho's hand shakes as he pours another.

"I needed a job."

"Yes, but..."

"It's complicated."

I start feeling like that innocent boy-man I once was, running on the road from Nebaj. I am looking for black-and-white answers to life from a man who spent 20 years fighting for a black-and-white answer until reality ended the revolution and he came down the mountain to live in a world of grays, where we all end up. But, I press on as if I were an investigative journalist hot on the trail of ultimate truth. There was a revolutionary party formed to give a political voice to ex-fighters. Why didn't he join that party?

"IT'S COMPLICATED!" he shouts, slamming down his empty glass. He fills it again as my head pulses. Who am I to stick a pin in someone who fought for his country 20 years in desperate situations and ended up with a broken body and nothing in hand when the gun fell from it. I thought of my broken heart when I returned from Guatemala and my girlfriend said she had another, but it was nothing compared to the death of a cause and the murder of a loved one. And when I got home, the resume I showed to prospective employers didn't begin with, "Work History: 1979-1994, Guerrilla."

"Come on, Pancho, let's go home."

As we wait for Uber, I steer the conversation to more genial matters and the tension goes away, as do the contents of the bottle. Uber arrives and we both got in. The driver was years younger than us and full of curiosity. When he discovered who Pancho was, he erupted with questions and Pancho exploded with answers. A 20-minute drive home turned into a 2 1/2 hour ramble through political history and Guatemala City. I handed a happy Pancho over to his eye-rolling wife and then spent another hour as the chatty driver pummeled me with questions. After midnight we finally pulled up to the hotel and he grabbed my hand like it was a well handle that he kept pumping.

"Thank you for the greatest night of my life," he said, and refused payment.

———

The next day, Casey awaited me at the airport.

"Dad!"

We clutched and spun around so joyfully that I expected applause from all the smiling people around us.. He seemed so big. Bigger even than his older brother. Not as tall as me but look at those broad shoulders.

"What was like for you, dad, when you went to Nicaragua?"

"I never did."

Hah! He had made his own path and took me step-by-step along it as we awaited our flight. What a story — of busing through Guatemala, Honduras and El Salvador to Nicaragua. The mountains, the rivers, the volcanoes, the people, the beaches, and the last day when he was warned to hide as the whole country hit the streets to celebrate the revolution's victory in 1979. Not a good day to be a citizen of a country seen as the revolution's enemy. When Casey finally ran out of story and breath, he turned to his iPhone to message his mother, and I turned to Google to type in a name that I had wondered about for decades. I didn't know whether to cry or yell when the results for *Morse Holladay* showed up. It wasn't so much that he had died 10 years after I left Cunén but about how he had lived before we met.

Morse was a war hero thrice-honored for bravery under fire during World War II and in Korea. He won the Navy Cross, second only to the Medal of Honor, for exposing himself to enemy fire to save his comrades from sure death. He won our country's third-highest honor, the Silver Star, for a similar act of bravery, and the Bronze Star for tossing a hand grenade to attract enemy attention to himself as others escaped. A hero....a true-hearted, life-tested stand-up guy who wore his honors inwardly.

I am surrounded by warriors and bravehearts — from the Melvilles of Maryknoll to the men and women of the neblina — Pancho and Tito and Hernan and Josue and...Ana.

Ana. As the loudspeaker calls our flight, I am already making plans to return and find Alejandra — not just to find out how her mother died, but how she had lived.

Finding Ana

2018

Ana's poem to her daughter

Ana's house

"I have found her!"

Alejandra's face instantly softens when Gaspar emerges from the neblina above where we waited on the slope of volcano Atitlan, and she gently sways her infant son left and right in a motion that soothes us all.

We thought Gaspar had been lost in that mysterious fog as he searched for Ana's secret resting place.

Alejandra's husband Mario — a powerful-looking, genial ex-guerrilla — smiles. My wife Laura, a photojournalist, readies her camera. I shiver, anticipating a climactic moment in my search for the mesmerizing woman I had met so many years ago on this volcano.

Last year, after learning that Ana had a daughter, I had spent weeks trying to set up this visit. It was a complicated process through family members and intermediaries, by email and Facebook and phone calls. It went slow for various reasons, including trust. The war ended in 1996, but not the suspicion, fear, hatred, killings, and kidnappings. When I finally broke through, Alejandra and the former guerrilla Tito met with me at a small hotel tucked away in Guatemala City. Here, on its private veranda, stories flowed for hours as exotic birds squawked in a nearby stand of trees where a fox played. I was content until a hotel employee about Alejandra's age pulled me aside.

"I hate those people."

Speaking in a low, hard voice, she revealed herself as the daughter of a retired army general, and not just any general but head of G-2 - the intelligence division responsible for so many deaths and disappearances during the war.

"These terrorists are killers."

Ahh, damn, I had encouraged Alejandra and Tito to speak openly about sensitive things they wanted no one else to hear, thinking this was a place without ears. Guilt and anxiety flushed through me, as well as twinges of old fear, but why am I surprised? Guatemala is never what it appears to be unless you stay at postcard distance as I was on that night of blissful ignorance when I ran with a happy heart into a full moon rising over the mountain's edge. You cannot reach into the picture and caress its beauty without feeling its thorns.

We moved our interviews to private homes, to cafes where we talked furtively, and, finally, to here on the volcano where Alejandra describes what it was like to be a little girl desperately waiting for mom to come down this very slope...to come home.

———————————

She was only five when Ana left to go up the mountain in 1982, the year G-2 unleashed security forces on ORPA safe houses throughout Guatemala City, killing Pancho's older brother. He held off soldiers as other militants escaped. A front-page picture in the newspaper Prensa Libra showed his bullet-torn body on the roof with an automatic weapon at his fingertips. Panic swept the capital and families feared for their lives, especially militant families like Ana's, whose women were collaborators. They hunkered down in their apartment until the day America's boyfriend, leader of the urban front, disappeared. He had warned them to flee if it happened.

Ana, sensing the snake was closing in, took the ultimate step up the mountain, as Alejandra's father Marco had done two years earlier. The rest of the family escaped Guatemala, eventually ending in Washington, DC. After the war, a newspaper story in Prensa Libra proved how right Ana's instincts had been. The story was based on secret police archives recently made public. The police had created index-type cards of those they killed or targeted. One of them was Ana. The information came from a guerrilla spy.

"It was shocking what they had about her — age, weight, height," Alejandra said. "They knew she had a child with Marco, that she was a capitana with ORPA, that her daughter, me, lived with her sister, America, and that she had bad knees. A note said she never made mistakes. Fortunately, *they* did. They had the wrong last name."

The family had saved itself, but a wounding rupture of time and space began opening. It lasted nearly 10 years during

Ana's time as a guerrilla leader, eased by a few surprise visits and secretive messages.

"Do not come up the mountain to be a guerrilla," Ana warned her sister in one cryptic note. "It is very difficult for a woman."

The first visit came three years later, four months after I met Ana on the volcano, at Christmas, and Alejandra's voice softened in telling about it.

"My grandmother said a friend was coming from Alaska. We went to the airport and two cousins paced nervously. Then I saw my uncle coming back with his arm around someone."

Mom.

Alejandra raced across the airport as Ana knelt and they melted into each other's arms, and wept.

"Mi hija — my daughter," Ana murmured into her ears and hair and face and heart.

Everyone laughed when Ana explained how she had gotten there. First, she slipped into Mexico and traveled to the border crossing at Tijuana, hoping she could pass as a tourist. She was pale-skinned, unlike the usual person from Mexico or Central America, and her big eyes were not the "O's" of frightened immigrants, nor would they have looked away as men in uniforms approached. She carried a colorful, over-size piggy bank that only American tourists would buy.

"Did you have a good time in Mexico, miss?" a border patrol agent asked.

"Yes," Ana said, as she strode across the boder — a revolution leader unwittingly welcomed into Ronald Reagan's paranoid United States. Her grandmother awaited and they flew to DC where for 10 days mother and child hung out in the apartment, barely leaving. They talked, watched TV, talked. Catching up. Making bonds they never had before. Getting to know each other. Just saying things and touching and being in each other's presence.

On the eleventh day, Alejandra woke to discover mom had left in the night. No last words. No goodbye hug for a little girl suddenly lost and lonely again.

Two years later, Ana met the family in Mexico City.

"It was wonderful. My mom stayed a month. We went to museums, she showed me the Aztec displays and taught me about them."

And then, again, she was gone.

Two more years passed. It was 1989, the year before peace talks began. A civilian president had been elected and the revolution was in stalemate. By now, Ana's sister America was deeply involved with a human rights group in DC and working with Rigoberta Menchu. Through her, they contacted Ana on the volcano by secretive means and the whole family reunited at the Mexican border town of Tapachula, the crossing for most of today's immigrants, and celebrated Alejandra's 13th birthday. Happy, happy, happy.

Ana disappeared.

A year later, Ana was ill when she suddenly showed up in Mexico City where Alejandra was living with some family members. Ana's thin body had shrunk further, she walked on painful knees, and suffered from anemia.

She was pregnant with Pancho's child.

Francisco, born in October, instantly soothed Alejandra's bruised heart, and for three months she reveled in the love of him and of Ana, but her grandmother, who had moved back to Guatemala, insisted that she come and finish school. It was harsh being under her rough thumb as Alejandra yearned for a real mother, but when she finally returned from school, mom had gone back up the mountain to say goodbye to the fighters she had mothered for so many years. After a month, she returned under a new assumed name, Rosalba Rodriguez, and took over a Mexican-based group that provided funds and other resources to ORPA. It was time, she said, to settle down. Thrilling news! Alejandra was almost 15, the most important year for a Latin American girl, the symbolic year of passing out of childhood.

Meanwhile, Pancho had been dipping in and out of the revolution, splitting time between being a comandante and getting repaired. He had suffered near-disabling injuries — the worst when he was fleeing soldiers, jumped off a cliff, and landed in a tree, broken, where compañeros rescued him two days later. A long, recuperative trip to Cuba and other places kept him away for months at a time, leaving the front in the hands of Santiago, the tall, unsmiling fellow next to Pancho in the portrait on his wall.

Here is where the virtues of life on the mountain sharply contrast with those of flatland normalcy. You may be married down there in normalville, but up here your spouse is the revolution and — as both Pancho and Ana told me on my first night in camp — sex is only sex, like hunger. Choose who you will. Man or woman or both. Under the ideals of the revolution, you are a free agent, free outside of your vows to la lucha. A 15-year-old guerrillera, the age at which girls down there had a birthday quinceañera, had multiple partners up here. And why not? She may not live to be 16. It was the kind of thing men do down there. Up here, we are all equal, the girl said, Pancho said, Ana said.

Tito remembers how Ana would come to him and talk after she and Santiago became a couple in Pancho's absence. She wasn't sure he would return and life is so short, especially up here. "She had the need to be human, to be loved. She had the same hungers as everyone. All of your humanity comes out when you are on the border of life and death."

Pancho and Ana reunited after he returned and, by what Tito observed, Santiago was sad but not angry. "He was very mature and understanding." Nor was there apparent conflict between Santiago and Pancho.

"These kinds of problems don't mean as much on the mountain."

But Tito, ever the empath, was no mind reader and could not know what Santiago and Pancho would reveal in the books they wrote after the war: that they intensely disliked each other, in part because of Ana, but also because they differed over how to lead guerrillas as time wore on without progress in the revolution. Eventually, everything was left in Santiago's hands when Pancho and Ana went down the mountain and struggled with normal life.

Ana, at 35, the veteran leader of men and women, seemed ill-equipped to handle children.

"My mother was so strange. Once, I was leaning on her when watching TV and she shrugged me away, saying, 'You know why I came down the mountain? It's because I don't want to carry other people anymore.'

Pushed aside or, worse, simply neglected by a mother she had yearned for all her life was crushing, but Alejandra would not give up. "I loved her. All we needed was more time."

When Francisco was born, so too was the chance for Ana to improve mothering skills and, as with everything else when she applied willpower, she seemed to be succeeding. The daughter with so many questions and needs for direction began getting a mother who answered and guided.

But there was a problem.

"She always defended Pancho. I hated her for that. I hated the figure of him being a partner with my mother. I wanted to be with my real father, Marco." She hadn't seen the sweet, gentle man since she was five. Thank God for Panchito, the baby's nickname. "He was something special for me. I always wished for a brother or sister, a company for all the time I was alone. Panchito was what I wanted. Love."

A family was finally coalescing against ridiculous odds

Ana and son

The Death of Ana

Gaspar leads us up an ever-steeper, wilder trail past orderly plantings of corn and coffee and avocado into a wilderness of brush and trees so dense that even the fog has a hard time penetrating. I ran through this kind of thicket as a young man and can barely walk through it now, largely because a few days ago I had climbed the great volcano San Pedro looming behind us and ruined what was left of the crumbling knee that had kept me out of Vietnam. It was foolish but I was determined to look upon nearby volcano Atitlan from a height. A guide pushed me from behind, urging many times, "Tu puedes, Terry" — you can. I appreciated his words, but it was Ana's that drove me: "Ni un paso atras" — not one step back. I repeated the phrase dozens of times through gritted teeth until, finally, we reached the summit, where guide books promised views from sea to sea, but on this day the heartless neblina poured over us like pancake batter and we could see nothing.

Now, as we struggle to keep up with Gaspar's nimble feet, Alejandra speaks about the most terrible day of her life.

"The day before mom died, Pancho, me, mom, and the baby went to a place in Mexico she liked — Morelos, where there is a big mountain everyone climbs. We didn't climb." She looked at me with a knowing grin that I instantly understood. Why go up the mountain if you don't have to? Then she sighed and spoke of how her dream at last was coming true.

"We were very happy that day as Pancho made delicious spaghetti and mom talked about her plans to stay in Mexico, have a place of our own, and raise us."

Ana also spoke of going the next day to meet a woman named Andrea, an ORPA collaborator who had been been avoiding Ana's attempt to clarify irregularities in ORPA's bank account.

Had Andrea been stealing? Or was it Ana, as Santiago suggested in his memoir?

Ana went alone to confront her — no big deal for a woman who once guided rockets against the army. They met at the bank, where records showed misappropriation of some kind. Ana and Andrea went to a parking garage, arguing loudly, witnesses said, and got into the woman's car. Andrea slid into the driver's seat as Ana opened the passenger door and turned to sit down.

Months later, during the murder trial, police presented damning evidence: a display of wicked daggers hung on the wall at Andrea's house, but one was missing. The one in Andrea's hand.

The dagger plunged into Ana's back, close to that formidable spine and deep into her left lung.

Ana staggered from the car.

The knife missed her heart, but not an artery, and Ana started bleeding to death. She was still alive when police arrived and asked who did it. "Robbers. We were robbed," Ana said, perhaps knowing that if she told the truth everyone in the rebel group including her family would be exposed.

Pancho got a call from a hospital in Mexico City: "Hurry, your woman is grievously wounded."

As he rushed to be with her, the smell of roses filled his car.

———

"This is the path Ana took," Gaspar says — the one she so often traveled from the guerrilla camp to the place we are headed. He knew Ana well and often came to that spot to absorb her teachings about having self-respect as a Mayan in a world ruled by powerful non-Mayans. He hasn't visited it for years and in his excitement runs ahead of us, once more disappearing as we catch our breaths.

"Up here," his voice urges.

The neblina opens its skirt to reveal Gaspar standing on the trail next to what must be the tallest tree on the volcano — a kind of long-trunk oak called a chicharo that soars like a redwood above the forest and clutches the earth with long, flaring, finger-like roots encircled by a wicked tangle of wild vines. This is the gathering place where Ana so often met with villagers, Gaspar says. Here is where the woman who had studied agronomy so that she could teach Mayans how to enrich their fields had found a classroom for teaching how to enrich their inner selves. And this is where she will meet visitors forevermore.

Alejandra pauses to rest and swallow tears.

"I cry every time I find her"

"My heart found out before they told me. I was at school and my heart started pounding. I couldn't breathe and my face changed color and everyone asked if I was ok. I went home, but as I walked I knew something was wrong. My mom hadn't picked up my brother. When I got home, a collaborator took me into the kitchen, sat me on a tall chair and told me."

Alejandra couldn't cry. She didn't comprehend. It was a bad dream. "I had just seen her alive that morning."

Pancho came home from the hospital.

"He was devastated. I saw it in his face and shrunken body. He collapsed."

She grabbed Francisco, who was not even two, and couldn't stop hugging him as tears started falling, They flowed throughout the funeral and for the next six months until the shock finally washed away. Twenty-five years later, she still cries at critical moments like this one.

"I cry every time I find her."

Alejandra settles upon the soft, green ground cover next to the tree and kisses her child. She is serene. No more tears. My wife's camera shutter clicks. Mario smiles. Everyone is so calm, so at peace, except me. I am poised for something ... mystical?

Suddenly, Gaspar throws out his arms, as if he were on the world's greatest stage, and cries out.

"THIS IS ANA'S HOUSE!"

His booming voice silences the birds, the camera, the cooing, the mystique.

The tree beckons and I move toward it, knowing that in the darkness of its tangled roots are the ashes of Ana, placed there by Gaspar 25 years before. I start pulling the vines apart to get closer...closer to a woman who had never died within me.

"Cuidado!"

I flinch backwards, feeling like a grave robber.

The vines are poisonous, Gaspar says, as if they were in collaboration with the mist to keep this place inviolate.

Alejandra speaks softly when I sit next to her.

"My mother used to write me little poems. The last one said: '*Look for me in places where I have been. If you find me there, you will know I did the right thing.*' I read and read and read that little scrap of paper until I lost it like I lost my mother."

It took years for Alejandra to understand its message and she wants me to understand it. Her gentle eyes, so warm and dark and like and unlike those of Ana, are as soft music accompanying her words.

"You are looking for my mother in the wrong place. Come."

As we retrace our steps, I realize that this isn't just the path Ana took to the village, it's the one she took down the mountain for the last time after saying goodbye to comrades she had led into battle, nurtured through terrible times, and encouraged when spirits lagged. She was the one who talked so many others out of leaving the guerrilla...*Stay...Keep the faith...The victory is coming...The people are counting on us... Ni un paso atras.*

Tito never went to the chicharon tree after her death. To him, she is not within tree roots but in his soul, as close to being a true love as he would ever get, the infinite love he dreamed of having as a child. "The love that remains far from my eyes, my skin, my words, but very close to my dreams." They were friends who shared secrets and jokes and gossip, and he so admired her bravery.

"You don't find that kind of woman twice in life. People like her come from the stars to do a task on this Earth and then those angels have to leave in some way. To go back."

The chicharo tree

Her Voice

The volcano spreads broadly at its base, where a pickup truck awaits us on the road to the village of Santiago Atitlan. Alejandra and her baby take the passenger seat while the rest of us clamber into the open truck bed — that is, they clamber while I struggle to swing my stiff and swollen leg on board and finally stand up behind the truck's cabin to enjoy the trip with my face into the wind. Back when I was hitchhiking home from my first trip to Guatemala and had lots of hair, I stood like this on a pickup, side-by-side with a companion on a warm night's ride through Mexico, screaming with joy as that hair snapped behind me at 70 mph. Suddenly, my friend flew backwards onto the truck bed, dazed with a dark wet spot between his eyes. I thought he'd been shot, but when I knelt to look closer, I saw the guts of a huge locust splattered on his forehead like it was a windshield. No such worries on this slow, rattling drive that lets me contemplate what happened in Santiago in 1990.

After 10 years of brutish army occupation, the village seethed. Its people, almost all Tzutujil Mayans known as Atitecos, had been suffering since the army first set up camp in 1980 just after ORPA fighters began appearing around the lake's edges. The hammer came down hard a year later with the army massacre of 16 villagers and the assassination of Catholic priest Stanley Rother. Over 1,000 villagers would die in other massacres over the years, but, since priests and Mayans were being slaughtered all over the country, Atitlan's woes were nothing special — until the night of Dec. 2, 1990 when 14 villagers, protesting peaceably over the wounding of a youth by drunken soldiers, were shot down by soldiers. International headlines and TV broadcasts spotlighted the horror and 15,000 villagers, out of 20,000, signed a petition demanding the removal of the army camp.

The outcry worked far beyond expectations. Guatemala's civilian president signed an order declaring Santiago an army-free zone, making it the only village in country history to kick out the army. Now we are headed toward a turnoff into that village to meet people who played a role in that victory, Gaspar's family. If we kept going straight, we would arrive at the village of Toliman where Father Greg had connected me with the guerrillas during the revolution, yet the army didn't bloody his village as it did Santiago, probably because he brought the army chief into his plans to buy — not seize — land and give it to local Mayans. Today, his parish has a self-supporting coffee cooperative that sells directly to customers around the world. Hence, Toliman is flourishing and its people stay put even as thousands of other Mayans flee coffee-producing areas like Huehuetenango, who cannot afford to grow coffee sold to international companies like Starbucks at depressed world prices.

Coming to Santiago as a guest is different than coming as a tourist. The tourist arrives by boat and is greeted at the dock by guides who want you to visit Maximon, the Mayan's version of a saint's statue. Candles flicker light upon his thin, wooden face, peering out from an encirclement of neck ties, with a cowboy-style hat down to his eyebrows and a cigar sticking out from his thin lips. You are encouraged to give him money and alcohol. The guerrillas did so in homage to the people's reverence for Maximon as devil and god. If you avoid Maximon, you walk upwards into the village through a corridor of vendors selling mostly hand-wrought traditional garments and hangings and art pieces and pottery. Eventually, you reach a small park dedicated to those killed in the 1990 massacre.

As special guests, we enter on a back street and twist through alley-sized roads into the heart of the village where people live unseen by tourists. The truck parks in front of a doorway that opens into a courtyard surrounded by rooms: a kitchen, bedrooms here and there, a dining room, and a room where a tv is playing a soap opera watched by a handsome woman dressed in the attire of the village. Elena, the younger sister of Gaspar, rises from the sofa to greet us with a bright open face. She wears the intricately embroidered blouse and wraparound skirt of her village and reaches for a trophy she was honored with for representing the essence of Mayan life. She is proud of her accomplishment and settles with a beaming smile upon the couch as her older sister Mercedes enters the room, wearing similar but more-worn clothing, and gently sits down at the far end of the couch — a clue to the opposite way she presents herself. Gaspar and Elena project outwards, but

Mercedes draws us inward as she answers the question of how Ana influenced her and the village.

"Ana?"

Her suddenly-trembling voice reveals a suddenly-full heart.

"I call her, 'The voice that came down the mountain and changed everything.' "

Her words, so unexpectedly profound, stagger me. Distrustful of my Spanish, I turn to Alejandra. "Did she say what I think? Can you interpret?" Alejandra asks her to explain.

In the late 80's, Ana would come to the chicharo tree to speak with villagers, meeting with them in ones and twos, sometimes in small groups who would settle upon the soft vegetation and listen. What they learned was so illuminating that they took its lessons back and taught others, who in turn spread *the word*. From person to person, family to family, the word replicated — *replicado* — throughout the village like a virus, transforming many into collaborators who provided food, coffee, information about the army, and even recruits to ORPA. I had met some of these in the guerrilla camp, fierce men and women and youth ready to join the cause. The word was about equality and self-worth and the true history of Maya people — the proud one before men on horseback took hold of their world.

The word went deep into the village psyche, and especially into their sense of themselves as human beings equal to all.

Ana wasn't the only guerrilla to bring the word, but no voice was more powerful than hers. As a woman she resonated with the women of Santiago, who like Mayan women everywhere were doubly oppressed because of their gender.

"She talked about our rights as humans, our rights as women, and that's what politicized me because at that time women were not equal to men. We weren't educated as men, we weren't allowed to have work," Mercedes said. Her education would have ended at 6th grade if Ana hadn't inspired her to get revolutionary. Barred from traditional brick-and-mortar education, she turned to education classes provided on the radio and got a bachelor's degree, as did every male and female child in the family.

"Ana was a woman prepared intellectually and her life was dedicated to the people, whose respect she earned. When I saw her come down the mountain the first time, I saw her bravery. She opened my eyes and made me love myself."

All five children became collaborators, not only supporting ORPA but spreading the equality word to others in the village and through the generations. Each generation heard and improved on the previous one. Gaspar's two daughters both had educations in traditional schools and speak better Spanish than him. Mercedes' nieces speak it much better than her.

The way Ana related to them, and her profound impact, was straight out of the pages of Bolker. Practical, so practical. She didn't teach down to the people of Santiago, Mercedes says, she put herself in their skin and invited them into hers.

"Ana loved other human beings — that is what made her special. And everything she did was out of that love. She didn't trade it for power or money or political gain. She gave it to us.

Her motive was that everyone have power. But to have power you had to have strength — the inner kind. Of believing you are as good as anyone."

Mercedes reenforced my belief that you can't see a ladder of opportunity until you believe it exists for you, too, and you can't climb it without an education that opens your eyes to your true place in history and, thence, to a future you are free to imagine and pursue. *Roosters again. Crowing and crowing and crowing in my memory as they had near Tito's house. As if they wanted to reenforce the message of equality, equality, equality.*

This is what the revolution wrought. It didn't change the government so much as it changed the governed. The peace accords signed in 1996 eliminated some of the structural barriers that had prevented Mayans from accessing the ladder; now it was up to the people to unite in a new revolution to seize democratically what had been seized from them autocratically. Ballots, not bullets.

Believe, Ana told them.

And one by one by one, they did.

There stand Elena and Mercedes — one displaying a trophy of proof, the other hugging herself as a trophy. One with a proud smile. One with grateful tears. And there stands Alejandra, gently swaying with Ana's grandchild at her bosom. She, too, has tears in eyes that draw me in as her mother's once did thousands of feet up there in the neblina.

"Do you remember my mother's poem?" Alejandra asks, and recites it.

Look for me in places where I have been. If you find me there, you will know I did the right thing.

"My mother is here," she says, pausing to let my heart comprehend the pain of a little girl left alone for years as the voice she yearned to hear spoke to others.

"She did the right thing."

Mercedes and Alejandra

An Epilogue of Hope

A year later, in 2019, my chicken bus chugged up the last steep stretch of road in the Cuchumatanes Mountains and leveled off at the high pass overlooking Cunén, where I saw it for the first time in four decades...and was stunned.

It was everywhere.

The village that once nestled in the palm of a valley was now so big it took up two or three handfuls. I almost couldn't see the old church because of all the new buildings, but the village's most prominent feature was still the cemetery, vast and glowing in the sun. My heart's ears heard the voice of village poet, don Paco: "So small a pueblo. So big a cemetery."

That's where you live, now, isn't it don Paco? I hope you have found a comfortable place to sleep with a nice blanket of fireflies to warm your soul at night.

After whispering a promise to visit him, I turned to see where true believers believe the Virgin of Candelaria appeared on the side of this road with a blast, but the driver was speeding and the windows were closed and dirty, so I decided to "look" for familiar things by feel — and immediately smiled as the bus made the big zig to reverse direction across the mountain and head down home. *Yes!* At just the right moment, just as

I remembered, the road flattened out, made a sweeping right turn upwards and hit a familiar bump. Ahhh, we were crossing the creek bridge. Someone opened the window on the far side, which let me see buildings streak by, and soon I expected to see the school I helped build, but instead the bus took a sharp right onto a road that never existed before into a flock of growling tuk-tuks that never before existed.

Don't go this way. I don't want to see people jump out of the way of traffic against so many new two- and three-story buildings. I want this smooth road to be bumpy like before. But it never existed before.

On we rambled through this unfamiliar place until the bus stopped and the attendant demanded I get out.

"But where is the church?"

"What church?"

"The Catholic church, the heart of Cunén."

"Up there in Los Trigales."

"No, the old one. In the center."

That? He pointed down a long, unfamiliar street I couldn't see the end of, then jumped atop the bus, threw down my backpack and whistled at the driver to get going. I barely had time to step aside, and would have cursed the bastard if not for the roar behind me.

A flood tide of tuk-tuks, heavily laden trucks, diesel-belching chicken buses, motorcycles, motor scooters and even a bicycle bore down upon me — filling the street curb to curb as they wrestled for position and honked-blared-tooted warnings that my life was in the hands of my feet. I leaped to the skinny little curb that acted as a sidewalk, hugged a building like my wife on our marriage night, and prayed that my protruding backpack would not be grabbed by a protruding truck mirror.

The pulse of traffic passed, leaving me smitten with a sad thought: Where's the village whose streets were full of people not beasts on wheels — people who ambled along and said *hola* in soft voices and smiled.

I felt like a stranger in this place that is like a small city; crippled by having the tiny streets of a village and a city's choking traffic. People weren't walking so much as hopping aside and quick-marching. Dogs did the dance, too, but they were more nimble, and didn't even turn around until the last second. A black dog stood insolently with his butt to the danger, looking for food with his ears straight up and twitching as they triangulated the threat and told him when to leap aside at just the last moment.

Something commercial was making this town grow, but it was not my mission to puzzle it out. I came here for a different story.

"Where's the village center - the old church?" I asked an old Mayan woman with a basket of tortillas balanced on her head. She steadied the burden with one hand and pointed with the other — a deeply brown, veined one with an arm far more muscled than mine.

"Down there to the right," her fluttering fingers said, as we both moved out of the path of a giant truck carrying concrete blocks to build this place even bigger.

Down there was a side street commandeered by the impolite tuk-tuks whose drivers call me 'jefe' as they streaked by. Jefe means boss, but they didn't sound respectful. Two more blocks of this took me to the town center and the church! Its cross and bells gleamed above the trees of the park, which was a parking lot for tuk-tuks lined up like a gauntlet to be run.

"Hola, jefe," said the drivers, lounging against their red beasties. Almost every one of the things had some religious insignia or picture of the virgin or words like, "My faith is in God."

I heard where the church is better than I could see it.

Chonk! Chonk! Chonk!

Even the angry tuk-tuks couldn't compete with the sound of men using heavy iron bars to break apart the concrete step where 14-year-old Juan Botón died of a soldier's bullet. The sight and sound of it kind of broke my heart. They were tearing apart my history and memories to rebuild it.

This hallowed place had been the town's center, its heart, and was so respected that never did you see even a corn husk upon its single, broad step that the old man Diego swept with his witch's broom. Not even the blood of the boy Juan Botón could be seen shortly after his killing, when I last came in 1985 and wondered where all the people were.

Now, this sacred place is squeezed by two-story structures. In 1972, half the village assembled in chairs, laughing at a movie projected upon its brilliant, whitewashed side. You'd think they were watching Daffy Duck cartoons, but it was a USAID documentary of the first moon-walk that had taken place just three years before. Aieee, 50 years ago now. 'Men walking on the moon? Ha, ha, ha. What a fine joke. The moon is our mother - the source of our lives, our corn, ourselves. Do you think our goddess would allow a skyrocket full of men to land upon her and perhaps penetrate her? We need more of these funny films to lighten our lives,' is how my memory heard their voices.

"Señor, do you need help?"

The strong, angular-cut face of a proud workman was looking at me as he leaned upon a 4-foot long wrecking bar. He was the color of rich soil.

"Yes, por favor, do you know a man named Botón? His son was killed by a soldier on these steps during the war."

"There are many who died in the conflict."

He had stiffened straight as that bar of his and his dark eyes were measuring me.

"He was a campesino, a Maya man."

"All of those killed here in the conflict were Maya."

"Yes, I know, but I am looking for just one."

He wanted me to go around to the rear of the church where, I think he said, there was a plaque dedicated to all the war dead. But I was not here to write about them all. Just one.

"Botón."

He shook his head and picked up his bar.

Chonk!

I turned away toward where the family lived in my memory. It was around the corner to the right, down the concrete street a block or so. A few young, jeans-wearing men were lounging in a tienda near where I thought the dwelling was. They were in their late teens or early 20s. Ah yes, this was probably the store where drunks were lounging as the funeral procession went by. One of the drunks had asked for money to buy cusha. I gave it to him and he headed back to this store as hundreds of villagers headed to the church with the body of Juan Botón on their shoulders.

"No, jefe, we never heard of a Botón before," the loungers said with some edge in their tone. "How old are you, jefe? You seem old."

Once the boys of this village tossed stones at me to test my mettle and when I threw them back much harder, they learned respect. These fellows were older and used words. I can throw words.

"How old are you — 10 or maybe 12? Have you learned your numbers yet? Can you count that high?"

The stone hit home and they all looked at each other sheepishly and shuffled their feet. I smiled, thinking, 'Terry, you still got arm.'

"Amigo, maybe I can help you."

A soft-bellied fellow of about 50 stood between me and the boys. With his curly black hair and kindly manner, he vaguely reminded me of don Paco.

"Botón? Si."

He led me across the street and up a ways next to the new two-story block building under construction, one of many new buildings taking over this no-longer-a-village-place named Cunén. Dodging a stream of tuk-tuks, we came to a worn gate-door with a 4-inch square hole at eye level. My benefactor started knocking.

"Botón? Botón?"

Through the peep hole I saw a young woman dressed in the ankle-length, traditional blue-patterned skirt of Cunén.

She opened the door, peering at us through eye glasses. She was solidly made with a fine, open, direct look and a confident smile.

"Botón?"

"Si, pase adelante."

She spoke with strength, introducing herself as Roxana.

I quickly explained my misssion: looking for the father of the son shot dead. Lastima, she said, he died last year and the mother two months ago.

Damn, I am too late.

"But my father Domingo is here — the other son of Juan Botón."

I caught my breath as she left to get him, the one whose existence had given the father hope.

Domingo, roused from a nap, came from his room looking tired, looking...familiar...a broad face with dark eyes and genial wrinkles that instantly awakened at my tale of having been at the steps of the church just after his brother died. I spoke of how, some days after the funeral, his father had approached me as I waited for the bus to take me away from Cunén, and I repeated his father's final words to me:

"Senor Terry, do you know about the Mayan social security system?"

"No."

"It is like this....A father works hard all his life, digging with a hoe in his steep field for food to feed his family and to sell so that he can save money to send a son to school. The boy leaves. One day, the father is bent over in the field and feels his son's hand upon his shoulder.

"'Get up, father. Drop your hoe. Come home. Sit in your chair. You have worked hard all your life for me. Now I will work hard for you.'"

The father turned and trotted away. He had so much hard work to do in the fields. There was one more son.

Domingo nodded.

"You are that son."

Domingo smiled.

"Come," he said and we walked back to the church so that he could pose for a picture near where the workman was pounding away the spot where his brother stood for the last time. Then we went to a little place with blue walls to talk and drink coffee.

Domingo has his father's eyes, but they are glittery, not the ones that left burn marks in me just before Juan walked back to the fields with his hoe to chop out some education for him.

"Domingo, you were your father's dream for the future. How did it work out?"

Nodding, thinking, looking out the door to the past for a long moment, he finally replied.

"I was educated in college and became a teacher, a third-grade teacher up there in Los Trigales." He waved toward the great, upward flowing land among the mountains named for the wheat that once colored it gold. Not so much wheat anymore on its mostly green slope. Onions grow there now, plus corn and other food items. A road cuts through it up the mountain where guerrillas once used its ridges and canyons at night for their road, navigating by the glow of Cunén's cemetery.

"How did your father die?"

Of ailments linked to a life of desperately hard work.

Sighing inwardly, I couldn't help but think he had died with pride in his heart for having done the right thing. But, Jesus, he lived to be 84! Domingo stood and signaled for a tuk-tuk. It's too long a walk to the cemetery, he said.

Too long? Why I remember walking in procession to the cemetery with hundreds of villagers. Isn't it just up there? No. It takes the speeding tuk-tuk minutes to deposit us at the cemetery gate. The driver is young and respectful and gets to keep the change.

———

If I had parachuted into this cemetery, and skipped seeing the town, I would have known that Cunén was no longer a humble village. Colorful homes for the dead flowed across my vision, rising high above the whitewashed adobe mounds. From the mountain top the cemetery still glowed white, but here at eye level the mounds were almost buried by blue/green/yellow/purple structures. They are made of block, like modern homes for the living. How prosperous this land of the dead has become. Deep within it, one of the most elegant homes was taller than me, its cross-peaked parapet looming above my head. In it were three graves one upon the other, each with gold embossed plates. Juan Botón's wife insisted that they all be buried together in this place and that she be on the bottom under her son and husband, whose apartments were bigger. The father's plaque read:

Your love was family, your passion work, your currency duty, your motto the truth and honesty

Domingo led me to the original place where his brother was buried. Just as I remembered, it was surrounded by humble white mounds.

"Do you remember, Domingo, that sad, rainy day when your little brother was placed inside and the workmen put bricks to close the door. And your father stood on a dirt mound here and raised his arms to the sky and cried out:

"My blood!

"My body!

"My bones!

"My people!

"My son!"

Domingo squinched his face at me, kind of nodding.

"My little brother."

"Do you remember, Domingo, how your father's voice softened when he looked at me and said:

"'We are all the same...those who are rich, those who are poor, those who are Indian, those who are ladino, those who are Norteamericanos. There is no difference among us. We are all the same. The man who shot the gun...The man who gave him the gun...The boy who was shot with the gun."

He nodded. "The army took the soldier away and we never heard if he was punished. He was one of theirs."

"One more thing, Domingo, did you know don Paco, the poet of Cunén?"

His face brightened.

"Everybody knew him, he was famous, he is here."

Of course he is here. All of his male family members had died around 50 — the age he was when I met him.

"How did he die?"

He tilted his thumb to his lips in a familiar gesture.

"Cusha."

He cannot know what fury raged in me at this news. Alcohol has slain or crippled so many friends of mine. It got my best friend Frank, it got Diego the dentist, it got Carlos the failed TB aide, and it almost got me. Aieee! It got the richest-hearted man I ever knew. Surely, he lives in a nice home here with a nice plaque telling something nice like what was written for Juan Botón. Or, maybe that verse he himself wrote:

"Oh, Cunén, hidden paradise, in your nights the stars appear as pearls, illuminating my tranquil and shining soul...You are a rest for every aching heart, a nest of love for all."

I should come back tonight and look at those pearls from this place that is more like his words than that busy place outside. I could stroll its little pathways, waiting for fireflies to arise.

"Aieee, no, Terry," Don Paco might whisper. "Fantasmas!"

Ah, yes, ghosts.

Of the past.

———————

Now, in the twilight, we were back home where Domingo's whole family gathered. I think it looked like it did the night of the funeral — that kitchen in the back corner where three women are slapping tortillas to a rhythm you want to dance to. But, no, wasn't the kitchen in a separate place? And it didn't have a shiny stainless refrigerator and gas stove.

"The funeral was next door at my parents' house," Domingo corrected me.

The family insisted that I sit in the honored head position at a long wooden table with all the family on both sides before me. After eating sweet tasting rolls of purple corn, I spoke of how I had come here after young Juan was killed, and repeated, with all the passion in my heart, the words of his father as he stood at the boy's grave; and of his words about the Indian social security system.

"How has it worked?" I asked them. "Did his dreams and hard work come true? He wanted to build something Mayans didn't have back then — a ladder for his family to climb out of the fields to a better life. A ladder to opportunity that Mayan people didn't have, especially women."

"It has worked well," said Roxanna, explaining with power and pride how she had benefitted.

Twice she was named queen of Cunén, not for posing in a bathing suit but for exhibiting the best qualities of a proud Mayan woman, fully rooted in the rich history of her people and fully poised to help her people move forward — adelante! She went on to the University of San Carlos, where Ana's ideas of equality had been hatched, and earned a degree. She works as an administrator for Save The Children, an international nonprofit organization, and is passionate about helping the poor children of her country.

The ex-guerrillero Geronimo was also passionate about children. They are why he decided to go up the mountain: "The children had no shoes." Very few Mayan people wore shoes then. Most men wore sandles handmade from old tire treads and strips of inner tubes. Most children and women wore nothing on their calloused feet. Now they all have shoes and women walk in them with a confidence I don't remember from before. They even ride motorcycles in their traditional long skirts, as drivers not just as passengers holding on to their man.

"Yes," said Roxana when I spoke of these things. "Maya people everywhere are rising. We don't look down as women used to do — we look up! We are a new generation of Maya women, educated and finding opportunities that weren't open to us before."

"Do you know Thelma Cabrera?"

"Of course!" she said with pride.

Thelma, a Maya woman from near the lake, had run for president in recent elections and finished a respectable fifth place. I am glad Roxana knows of her, but doubt she ever heard of the guerrilla captain whose name is captured within hers. It's a long way from the chicharo tree on volcano Atitlan to here.

"Let me tell you the story of a woman named Ana, who taught Mayan men and women about equality," I said, recounting how the women of Atitlan call her, "The voice that came down the mountain and changed everything."

Is it possible that Ana's voice traveled this far? It's a fanciful thought that evaporates as I recall the night so long ago when I stood up there on that high road and watched lightning burst in clouds atop volcano Atitlan — too far away to hear the thunder let alone Ana's soft-spoken words. Hers was one of many voices carried down the mountains of Guatemala by men and women speaking of equality — and fighting for it with guns and inspirational words.

As I mused, the brother spoke.

"Yes, we believe that we are equal and must fight for it." He is angry as he talks of a recent incident involving Mayans and the army. A state of siege has been imposed across the country. Another example of discriminatory treatment by the government, he believes. Only a few months ago, this firebrand started a Facebook news site about the village, surrounding villages and aldeas, and the country. He and his two sisters fill it with photos, news bits and video commentary. He is pretty good with that microphone. He reminded me of a don Paco with lightning in his belly.

Are you listening, do Paco, from your comfortable resting place? What do you think of this young fellow — do you approve?

Silence. The distance from here to the cemetery is even greater than from here to the volcano.

It was dark as the entire family walked me the half-mile back to my hotel. It was dark not just because the sun had fallen and not just because there were few streetlights. It was dark because there were so few vehicle lights. And it was quiet because there were so few vehicles. It was my old village of Cunén, again, as we strode along with our feet shuffling like whispers upon the concrete and stones, laughing at goofy things. Roxana and her sister Juana trailed behind Domingo and Juan and I, giggling and chirping and from the sound of it, dancing and spinning. Just one happy family, and me too, on as sweet a walk as ever I have taken.

We arrived, embraced, promised to remain friends forever. Then they disappeared back into the evening and I to my bed.

The new Cunén awakened me with a roar, and once more I danced around traffic before I could flag down a tuk-tuk for a ride up to the high pass to catch a bus.

The tuk-tuk stopped where the Virgin had appeared so I could take a picture of the village. There was no miraculous explosion here at this spot — it was actually blown out by roadbuilders using dynamite, just as the little miracle down there was chopped out by a man with heart and hope and a plan and a hoe. Like all miracles, his was rare. Hoes aren't magic wands. Many others throughout Guatemala are dropping theirs and fleeing to the United States where walls of concrete and steel and barbed wire and armed men and cages await.

So, here I stood on this road, about to leave Cunén for the third time. The first time, in 1973, I walked away whistling and composing a song. The second time, in 1985, I rode away in a chicken bus, mourning what I found. And now...a happy ending?

Nah. This is no fairy tale. A year later, in June, soldiers surrounded Juan Carlos Botón — who had become a local journalist — in front of the church where his uncle had been killed and stuck a pistol in his back as they beat him, threatening to kill him because he had taken pictures of them strolling around without masks despite a nationwide order that all people must be masked because of the covid virus. They acted as if they were above the law as soldiers in this country have always acted toward Mayans. Juan had a nervous breakdown, which is understandable when you consider what happened to his namesake uncle in 1985. As he recovered, a hurricane rose out of the Caribbean over the village, unleashing floods that washed away homes of more than 100 very poor people and all roads from the outside world. Abandoned as usual by their government, the people subsisted on supplies flown in by helicopter from El Salvador and by private help brought in by four-wheel-drive caravans. And to no one's surprise, Roxana Botón rallied villagers, using money I was able to raise from donors in the U.S., to rebuild 25 homes in six weeks — a marvelous Christmas present, although many more went without in a land where neglect had replaced guns as the weapon of oppression. Countrywide, more than 700,000 dropped their hoes and were caught at the U.S. border along with millions of others fleeing Latin America's lack of opportunities and surfeit of dangers linked to corruption, drugs and gangs.

And yet, a bright spot of hope emerged in 2023 as Mayans who stayed home united in a new political party called Semilla (the seed) and — to the astonishment even of themselves — elected a president named Arévalo. Sound familiar? He's the son of Guatemala's first democratically elected president whose reforms 75 years ago so frightened U.S. interests that they faked a revolution that ended democracy and created a real civil war that left nearly 200,000 Mayans dead. Arévalo Jr.'s overwhelming win shocked elites who had run the country to suit themselves since then. It was as if 60 percent of the country had crowded into don Don Paco's bus, put Arévalo in the driver's seat, and drove into a valley of glowing luciernegas. And who could not feel, as Bernardo Arévalo took office in 2024, that Martin Luther King's arc of justice had finally rainbowed across Guatemala after three-quarters of a century?

Of course, a voter's mandate is not a magic wand anymore than the hoe Juan Botón picked up after leaving the cemetery; it is a chance for Mayan people to have a powerful role in reshaping a land taken from them hundreds of years ago, and it will take tough political hoeing to create the kind of equitable change whose success may be measured over years and by the number of feet walking north.

Acknowledgements

A huge hug to Margarita Melville, whose life and good works should encourage all who care about injustice and underdogs. Thanks to Jean-Marie Simon, who introduced me to various key people such as Ana's daughter, and whose work in Guatemala is historic; to "Comandante Pancho" and other ex-guerrilleros, including Tito "Capitan Julio" who gave me extensive interviews and helped design this book; and Rafael Ugarte, nephew of Ana.

Special thanks to Harris Done, who encouraged me to discover the Mayan people by inviting me to be a volunteer with his group, AYUDA. His group, like so many in Central America, does the kind of unglamorous hands-on work that gets lost in headlines about gangs, murder, corruption, and migrant caravans. By working shoulder-to-shoulder with people living in poverty, I learned why some leave, most stay, and how invisible they are whose dark-to-dark labor brings coffee and vegetables to the lips of people like me who live *al norte*. In that regard, abrazos to the Botón family for welcoming me into their family after so many decades — they are exemplars of how dreams are made when ladders of opportunity are offered.

Thanks, also, to my own adventurous family, who accompanied me on research trips to Guatemala, and have been so supportive in this project. Gracias, *mis queridas*: Laura, Edan, Casey, and uncle Steve.

No author publishes without input from other writers and editors, and this book would have failed without support from Michael Meenan, Paul McHugh, and Mary Jo McConahay.

Bibliograpghy

Aside from personal experience, I immersed myself in personal interviews, anthropological studies, scholarly papers, news articles, and many books dealing with the Cold War, Central America, South America, Mexico, Cuba, revolution, and migration. Highly recommended are the following books that provided depth, breadth, and background to my writing:

La Patria del Criollo: An Interpretation of Colonial Guatemala, Severo Martínez Peláez, 2009

Insurgentes Guatemala, La Paz Arrancada, Santiago Santa Cruz Mendoza, 2004

Sierra Madre, Pasajes y Perfiles de La Guerra Revolucionaria, Pedro Pablo Palma Lau, 2010

El Insurrecto Solitario, Vida Y Obra De Marco Antonio Flores, J.l. Perdomo Orellana, 1997

Solito, a memoir — Traveling alone at age 9 from war-afflicted El Salvador through Central America and Mexico to the U.S., Javier Zamora, 2022

What You Have Heard Is True, a Memoir of Witness and Resistance, Carolyn Forche, 2020

The War for the Heart and Soul of a Highland Maya Town: Revised Edition, Robert Carlsen, 2011

Guatemala, Eternal Spring — Eternal Tyranny, Jean-Marie Simon, 1987

Between Two Armies In The Ixil Towns of Guatemala, David Stoll, 1993

Guerrillas of Peace, Liberation Theology and The Central American Revolution, Blase Bonpane, 1985

Imagine No Religion, Blase Bonpane, 2011

Whose Heavan, Whose Earth, Thomas and Marjorie Melville, 1971

Through A Glass Darkly, The U.S. Holocaust in Central America, Thomas Melville, 2005

Time Among The Maya, Ronald Wright, 1991

Central America's Forgotten History, Aviva Chomsky, 2021

Maya Roads, Mary Jo McConahay, 2011

Ricochet, Two Women War Reporters and A Friendship Under Fire, Mary Jo McConahay, 2014

Silence On The Mountain, Daniel Wilkinson, 2002

I, Rigoberta Menchu, edited by Elisabeth Burgos-Debray, 1984

The Guatemalan Military Project, A Violence Called Democracy, Jennifer Schirmer, 1998

Guerrilla Warfare, Ernesto "Che" Guevara, 2012 edition

Overthrow, America's Century of Regime Change From Hawaii To Iraq, Stephen Kinzer, 2006

Bitter Fruit: The Story of the American Coup in Guatemala, Revised and Expanded (Series on Latin American Studies) Stephen Kinzer/Stephen Schlesinger, 2005

The Line Becomes A River, Dispatches From The Border, Francisco Cantú, 2018

Masacres de La Selva (Ixcan, Guatemala), Ricardo Falla, 1992

Inevitable Revolutions, The United States in Central America, 2cnd edition, Walter La Feber, 1994

The End of The Myth, From The Frontier To The Border Wall In The Mind of America, Greg Grandin, 2019

Escaping The Fire, Tomas Guzano and Terri Jacob McComb, 2010

Open Veins of Latin America, Five Centuries of The Pillage of a Continent, Eduardo Galeano, 1997

The Guatemala Reader, Edited by Greg Granadin, Deborah T. Levenson, Elizabeth Oglesby, 2011

Here We Are — American Dreams, American Nightmares, Aarti Namdev Shahani, 2019

The Art of Political Murder: Who Killed The Bishop?, Francisco Goldman, 2007